Teaching
Contemporary
British Cinema

Sarah Casey Benyahia

Series Editor: Vivienne Clark
Commissioning Editor: Wendy Earle

bfi Education

British Library Cataloguing-in-Publication Data
A catalogue record for this book is available from the British Library

ISBN 1 84457 061 4

First published in 2005 by the British Film Institute
21 Stephen Street, London W1T 1LN

With additional thanks to Peter Todd, *bfi* National Library, for advice

Design: Amanda Hawkes
Cover photograph: *courtesy of bfi* Stills
Printed in Great Britain by: Cromwell Press Ltd

www.bfi.org.uk

The British Film Institute's purpose is to champion moving image culture
in all its richness and diversity across the UK, for the benefit of as wide
an audience as possible, and to create and encourage debate.

Contents

Introduction to the series

Since the introduction of the revised post-16 qualifications (AS and A2 Level) in the UK in September 2000, the number of students taking A level Film and Media Studies has increased significantly. For example, the latest entry statistics show the following trend:

Subject & Level	June 2001	June 2002	June 2004
A Level Film Studies †	2017	-	-
AS Level Film Studies	3852	-	7996
A2 Level Film Studies	-	2175	4161
A Level Media Studies* †	16,293	-	-
AS Level Media Studies*	22,872	-	30,745
A2 Level Media Studies*	-	18,150	22,746

*Three combined awarding bodies' results
† Legacy syllabus – last entry June 2001
(source: *bfi* Education website – AS/A2 statistics refer to cashed-in entries only)

In September 2005, a new A Level specification (syllabus), Moving Image Arts (offered by the Northern Ireland awarding body, CCEA), will be available in the UK and it is likely to attract even more students to this lively and popular subject area.

Inevitably this increase in student numbers has led to a pressing demand for more teachers. But, given the comparatively recent appearance of both subjects at degree level (and limited availability of specialist post-graduate teaching courses), both new and experienced teachers from other disciplines are faced with teaching these subjects for the first time, without a degree level background to help them with subject content and conceptual understanding. In addition, these specifications saw the arrival of new set topics and areas of study, some of which change frequently, so there is an urgent need for up-to-date resources to help teacher preparation, as well as continuing professional development courses.

I meet a large number of Film and Media Studies teachers every year, in the course of my various roles, and developed the concept and format of this series with the above factors, and busy and enthusiastic teachers, in mind. Each title provides an accessible reference resource, with essential topic content, as well as clear guidance on good classroom practice to improve the quality of teaching and students' learning. We are confident that, as well as supporting the teacher new to these subjects, the series provides the experienced specialist with new critical perspectives and teaching approaches as well as useful content.

The two sample schemes of work included in Section 1 are intended as practical models to help get you started. They are not prescriptive, as any effective scheme of work has to be developed with the specific requirements of an assessment context, and ability of the teaching group, in mind. Likewise, the worksheets provided in the online materials offer examples of good practice, which can be adapted to your specific needs and contexts. In some cases, the online resources include additional resources, such as interviews and illustrative material. See www.bfi.org.uk/tfms.

The series is clear evidence of the range, depth and breadth of teacher expertise and specialist knowledge required at A Level in these subjects. Also, it is an affirmation of why this subject area is such an important, rich and compelling one for increasing numbers of 16- to 19-year-old students.

It has been very gratifying to see that the first titles in this series have found an international audience, in the USA, Canada and Australia, among others, and we hope that future titles continue to be of interest in international moving image education.

Every author in the series is an experienced practitioner of Film and/or Media Studies at this level and many have examining/ moderating experience, or is a industry professional. It has been a pleasure to work closely with such a diverse range of committed professionals and I should like to thank them for their individual contributions to this expanding series.

Vivienne Clark
Series Editor
November 2004

Key features

- Assessment contexts for the major UK post-16 Film and Media Studies specifications
- Suggested schemes of work
- Historical contexts (where appropriate)
- Key facts, statistics and terms
- Detailed reference to the key concepts of Film and Media Studies
- Detailed case studies
- Glossaries
- Bibliographies
- Student worksheets, activities and resources (available online) – ready for you to print and photocopy for the classroom.

Other titles available in the series include:

Teaching Scriptwriting, Screenplays and Storyboards for Film and TV Production (Mark Readman);
Teaching TV Sitcom (James Baker);
Teaching Digital Video Production (Pete Fraser and Barney Oram);
Teaching TV News (Eileen Lewis);
Teaching Women and Film (Sarah Gilligan);
Teaching World Cinema (Kate Gamm);
Teaching TV Soaps (Lou Alexander and Alison Cousens);
Teaching Contemporary British Broadcasting (Rachel Viney).

Forthcoming titles include:

Teaching Music Video; *Teaching Auteur Studies*; *Teaching Men and Film*; *Teaching Analysis of Film Language and Production*; *Teaching Video Games*; *Teaching Film Censorship and Controversy*; *Teaching Stars and Performance*; *Teaching TV Drama*
For details of these titles go to: www.bfi.org.uk/tfms

SERIES EDITOR: Vivienne Clark is a former Head of Film and Media Studies and an Advanced Skills Teacher. She is currently an Associate Tutor of *bfi* Education and Principal Examiner for A Level Media Studies for one of the English awarding bodies. She is a freelance teacher trainer and writer/editor, with several published textbooks and resources, including *GCSE Media Studies* (Longman 2002) and *Key Concepts & Skills for Media Studies* (Hodder Arnold 2002). She is also a course tutor for the *bfi*/Middlesex University MA level module, An Introduction to Media Education, and a link tutor and visiting lecturer for the Central School of Speech & Drama PGCE (Media with English), London.

AUTHOR: Sarah Casey Benyahia is a lecturer in Film and Media Studies with experience of teaching on a range of further and higher education courses at A level, BTEC and degree level. She is also a Principal Examiner for one of the English awarding bodies.

1

Introduction

Assessment contexts

	Awarding body & level	Subject	Unit code	Module/Topic
✓	AQA AS Level	Media Studies	Med 1	Reading the Media
✓	AQA AS Level	Media Studies	Med 2	Textual Topics: Film and Broadcast Fiction
✓	AQA A2 Level	Media Studies	Med 4	Texts and Contexts
✓	AQA A2 Level	Media Studies	Med 6	Comparative Critical Analysis
✓	EdExcel AVCE	Media: Communication and Production	Unit 1	Analyse Media Products
✓	EdExcel	BTEC National Certificate/ Diploma in Media	Unit 37	Film Studies
✓	OCR AS Level	Media Studies	2731	Textual Analysis
✓	OCR AS Level	Media Studies	2732	Audiences and Institutions
✓	OCR A2 Level	Media Studies	2734	Critical Research
✓	OCR A2 Level	Media Studies	2735	Media Issues and Debates Topic: British cinema since 1990
✓	OCR AVCE	Media	7400	Film Studies
✓	WJEC AS Level	Film Studies	FS1	Making Meaning 1
✓	WJEC AS Level	Film Studies	FS2	Producers and Audiences
✓	WJEC AS Level	Film Studies	FS3	Messages and Values
✓	WJEC A2 Level	Film Studies	FS4	Making Meaning 2
✓	WJEC A2 Level	Film Studies	FS6	Critical Studies: Section B, Producers and Audiences, Section C, Messages and Values

Awarding body & level	Subject	Unit code	Module/Topic
✓ SQA Higher	Media Studies	D332	12 Media Analysis
✓ SQA Advanced Higher	Media Studies	D332	13 Media Analysis
✓ SQA Advanced Higher	Media Studies	DF14	12 Media Analysis (Fiction)
✓ SQA Advanced Higher	Media Studies	D37A	13 Media Investigation
✓ SQA Advanced Higher	Media Literacy	C01K	12 Media Investigation: Film
✓ CCEA AS Level	Moving Image Arts	AS1	Language: Film Genre
✓ CCEA AS Level	Moving Image Arts	AS3	Critical Analysis
✓ CCEA A2 Level	Moving Image Arts		Teaching from Sep 05

This guide is also relevant to the teaching of film in Lifelong Learning courses, such as BTEC National Diploma.

The following titles in this series would be useful companions to this guide:
- *Teaching Analysis of Film Language and Production* (forthcoming)
- *Teaching Scriptwriting, Screenplays and Storyboards for Film and TV Production*
- *Teaching World Cinema*
- *Teaching Auteur Studies* (forthcoming)
- *Teaching Stars and Performance* (forthcoming)

For updates on these and additional titles, see www.bfi.org.uk/tfms.

Other *bfi* resources which support this topic include:
- www.screenonline.org.uk – a comprehensive and engaging (free) resource for schools and colleges on all aspects of British cinema and television;
- *British Cinema in the 1960s* – a teaching guide on a CD-Rom by Wendy Hewing, focusing on the three British social realist films: *Saturday Night and Sunday Morning* (Karel Reisz, 1960), *A Taste of Honey* (Tony Richardson, 1961), *The Loneliness of the Long Distance Runner* (Tony Richardson, 1962);
- 16+ Study Guides on *Contemporary British Cinema* and *60s British Cinema* from the *bfi* National Library at http://www.bfi.org.uk/nationallibrary/collections/16+/

● Specification links

The study of British cinema is appropriate to the following specifications. The relevant areas of the units are listed below, with a direct link to the section in the guide provided where necessary.

AQA AS Level Media Studies – Med 1: Reading the Media and A2 Level Media Studies Med 6: Comparative Critical Analysis

- Knowledge and application of key concepts: representation, audience, media language, values and ideology, institutions
- Textual analysis of unseen media texts

The guide provides analysis and application of the key concepts relevant to these units, and many of the student activities develop the skills of textual analysis relevant to discussing unseen media texts.

AQA AS Level Media Studies – Med 2: Textual Topics in Contemporary Media – Film and Broadcast Fiction

- Close study of two contemporary films
- Evaluation of film and media language
- Issues of representation, narrative, institution (non-Hollywood)

The case studies can be used as a basis for the Film and Broadcast fiction topic. (Case study 1 relates to film style and genre; Case study 2 relates to representation; Case study 3 relates to institutions.)

AQA A2 Level Media Studies – Med 4: Texts and Contexts

- Representation; particular groups and places in film
- Genre; the thriller

Case study 1 relates to realism and the thriller; Case study 2 relates to representation of refugees; Case study 3 relates to representation of England.

AQA A2 Level Media Studies – Med 6: Comparative Critical Analysis

- Knowledge and application of key concepts: representation, audience, media language, values and ideology, institutions
- Comparative critical analysis of two (or more) unseen media texts.

Section 2: Background outlines the key debates in audience, ideology and representation.

EdExcel AVCE Media: Communication and Production (single and double awards) – Unit 1: Analyse Media Products

- Representation
- Genre analysis
- Narrative structure

EdExcel (4351, 4355) BTEC National Certificate/Diploma in Media – Unit 37: Film Studies

- Textual analysis
- Investigate current issues and debates in film
- Investigate independent and mainstream film audiences

Section 2: Definition and discussion of the role of national cinema.

OCR AS Level Media Studies – Unit 2731: Textual Analysis
- Technical aspects of moving image (unseen analysis)

OCR AS Level Media Studies – Unit 2732: Audiences and Institutions
- Media ownership; processes of production and distribution

Section 1: British film abroad; Case study 3 deals with distribution, and an analysis of Working Title.

OCR AS Level Media Studies – Unit 2734: Critical Research
- Women and Film; representation of gender

Section 1: Representation; Case study 3 looks at the films of Gurinder Chadha.

OCR A2 Level Media Studies – Unit 2735: Media Issues and Debates
- Section B: British cinema since 1990

OCR AVCE Media: Film Studies 7400
- British film, national cinema, film language

WJEC AS Level Film Studies – FS1: Making Meaning 1
- Form and style, narrative and genre

WJEC AS Level Film Studies – FS2: Producers and Audiences
- Finance, production, distribution, national cinema

Section 1: Role of the Film Council, Case study 3 deals with FilmFour and Working Title.

WJEC AS Level Film Studies – FS3: Messages and Values
- Representation, comparative studies
- Close study films: *My Son the Fanatic*, *Sweet 16*

WJEC A2 Level Film Studies – FS4: Making Meaning 2
- Auteur Research Project

Section 3: Case studies on the directors, Gurinder Chadha, Stephen Frears, Michael Winterbottom.

WJEC A2 Level Film Studies – FS6: Critical Studies – Section B Producers and Audiences
- Issues and debates
- Indigenous film production
- Independent film and its audience

Section 1: What is British cinema for? Case study 1: *Last Resort*, *In This World.*

WJEC A2 Level Film Studies – FS6 Critical Studies: Section C
Messages and Values
- Film interpretation
- Social and cultural studies

Case study 1 deals with representations of gender, class, refugees; Case study 3 deals with British Asian and Black British cinema.

SQA Higher/Advanced Higher Media Studies

D332 12 Media Analysis
- Analysis of a range of media texts including film

D332 13 Media Analysis
- Narrative, representation audience, institution

D37A 13 Media Investigation
- Choice of film topic investigated with reference to representation, ideology, institution

DF14 12 Media Analysis (Fiction)
- Analysis of film, covering film language, narrative, representation, audience, institution

C01K 12 Media Investigation: Film
- Research into the film industry with reference to products and production process

CCEA AS Level Moving Image Arts

AS1 Language: Film Genre

AS3 Critical Analysis
- Analysis of production context, film language, audience, representation for reading and understanding film

Past exam questions from AQA, OCR and WJEC exam boards are available online at www.bfi.org.uk/tfms.

Getting started: Teaching contemporary British cinema

This section outlines the main areas of study, demonstrates the links between the subject area and film and media key concepts, suggests strategies for teaching and lists useful resources. The final part of the section places the debates about British cinema within the context of academic approaches and definitions (see p 14 Approaches and perspectives used to define British cinema).

The following discussion points illustrate the key issues that should structure any study of British cinema. Relevant sections in the guide are indicated but it is also important to remember that these ideas underpin the guide as a whole.

The term 'contemporary' in the title effectively refers to films produced since 1990, given that they are likely to be accessible to students, as the cultural and political contexts of the 1990s are not too distant from those of today. It is hoped that, armed with the key issues, debates and contextual information provided, teachers will encourage students to relate what they have studied to very recent and current films and film industry developments. Where appropriate, reference is made to films and events from earlier decades.

● Key questions for students

● Is there a definition of British cinema on which we can all agree?

Many different criteria have been used to define British cinema, including funding and subject matter. See p23 What is a British cinema for?, p24 The role of the Film Council.

● What does the term 'British' mean in this context?

Is it possible to discuss a single concept of Britishness without considering individual nations and regions? Has the term 'British' become a synonym for 'English'? See p31 National identity.

● Is it important for Britain to have a film industry?

Within the context of multimedia conglomerates (eg Time Warner, News International) and globalisation, does it matter if Britain (and by implication other nations) has a film industry? If there were no British films would this have a cultural and economic effect on British audiences and/or business? The influence of Hollywood is particularly relevant to British cinema due to a shared language and culture; the effect of this will be explored through issues of funding, distribution and audience choice. See p34 British film abroad, and p74 Case study 3: British cinema and institutions.

● What part does British film play in analysing and reflecting British culture?

British films are often seen as part of a national culture, and as playing an important role in constructing concepts of national identity. Is it important for films to tell culturally specific stories about the British? See p23 What is British film for? and p59 Case study 2: British Asian cinema.

● What does a British audience want from British cinema?

Given the range of audience groups (different ages, races, cultures, genders; different reasons for going to the cinema in the first place) this is a difficult question. British films tend to be characterised either as representing our own culture (whose culture?) and experiences in a realist style, or as genre films providing comedy and escapism. Does it always have to be a choice between the two? See p43 Case study 1: Social realism since 1990.

● How should British cinema be funded?

Can British film be defined as an art form, which should be protected from market forces by the donation of public money? Or should British cinema operate more like Hollywood, where decisions of funding are made on the basis of predictions of future commercial success? See p24 The role of the Film Council, p74 Case study 3: British cinema and institutions.

● The role of British television

The influence of broadcasting on film production includes successful film spin-offs from television programmes, funding for production (BBC Films and formerly, FilmFour) and a means of distribution. Television's role in representing the nation through a range of genres also raises questions about what audiences expect of home entertainment and consequently at the cinema. See p38 Realism, p74 Case study 3: British cinema and institutions.

● Why teach British cinema? A rationale for teachers

British cinema provides an opportunity to explore all of the key concepts in Film and Media Studies:

● Film and media language

Conventions of genre and film styles, including social realism, drama documentary. See p51 *Dirty Pretty Things* and the thriller genre, p57 *In This World* and drama documentary, and p38 Realism.

● Institutions

The way in which decisions about funding, production, distribution and exhibition affect the kinds of films that are made and seen. See p34 British film abroad, p59 Case study 2: British Asian cinema (Black Audio Film Collective) and p74 Case study 3: British cinema and institutions (FilmFour and Working Title).

● Audiences

Audience studies covers issues including marketing, demographic research, indentification and interpretation. See p35 *Four Weddings and a Funeral*, and p50 *Dirty Pretty Things* and characterisation.

● Representation

How films (and other media) construct images of particular groups (eg refugees, British Asian women), places (eg London, Margate) and nations; what forms these representations take and their cultural/historical context. See p78 Representation, p31 National identity and p20 Scheme of work 2: British cinema and representations of national identity.

◉ Messages and values; Ideology

Closely linked to the analysis of representation, the study of messages and values and ideology requires students to recognise the way that films (implicitly and explicitly) comment on society, often challenging dominant points of view. See p29 Ideology, p43 Case study 1: Social realism since 1990.

◉ Keeping up with debates

Many of the central debates about the funding and aims of British film are unresolved and students should be encouraged to respond to these issues as real debates and problems to be argued. For example British films receive government money, and the government has a duty to spend public money in the best interests of the British people. Who benefits from this money? The people who work in the industry? The audience? Should the money be awarded on the basis of a cultural imperative or to ensure a return at the box office? Filmmakers, actors, producers and viewers passionately hold different views on these issues, and it is important that students realise the relevance of these debates to contemporary life. See p23: What is British cinema for? and interviews with Chris Chandler (Film Council) and Alex Cox at www.bfi.org.uk/tfms.

While studying British cinema, students will be introduced to a range of films which might reflect or challenge their own experiences of British culture. Students need to recognise the ways in which films can analyse and dissect the world, in addition to their more familiar function as escapism and entertainment. The history of British cinema provides examples of competing representations of class, gender and race, vital for understanding not just the role of British film but also the wider society in which it exists.

● Research and resources

The following resources are very useful for keeping up-to-date with recent examples of British films and the debates around funding British cinema:

- ◉ **http://www.filmguardian.co.uk, and
  http://www.mediaguardian.co.uk**
  Printable versions of articles eg 'The Big Picture, British Film Special', Andrew Pulver 16/11/04, access through 'archive' on filmguardian.
- ◉ **The Department of Culture, Media and Sport (DCMS) Select Committee Report**
  This includes a legislative definition of British film, based on financial considerations, discussion of the problems facing the film industry and contributions from key industry figures. Available at: www.publications.parliament.uk/pa/cm/cmselect.htm (follow the link to Culture, Media and Sport). A summary of the statutory definitions and those produced by the British Council are available online at www.bfi.org.uk/tfms and can be used in conjunction with Worksheet 1 (see p13).

◉ *Sight and Sound*

This monthly film journal from the *bfi* includes reviews and features (eg May 2004, articles on tax breaks for British films and short film production and distribution).

You can also:

◉ Encourage students to keep a record of the British films that they watch at the cinema, on TV, DVD etc, which will provide a basis for their own research.

◉ Collect examples of current advertising campaigns in magazines (*Time Out*, *Empire*, *Total Film*, *Sight and Sound* etc) to use for textual analysis. Every current film has its own website with a link to trailers, clips, stills etc. Film posters are increasingly available online: www.imdb.com provides links under the merchandising section for each film. DVD and video covers can be used for analysing particular marketing campaigns. You can compare how different poster designs are used in different countries and discuss possible reasons for the differences.

Important note

◉ Television programmes are referenced, in parentheses, by which UK broadcast channel first aired the programme.

◉ All films referred to in this guide are presumed to be UK-produced, unless indicated, in parentheses, as by another country or as a co-production.

● Definitions of regional and national identity

(See p31 National identity, British cinema as national cinema.)

Students are likely to find discussions of national and regional identity challenging and it is useful to introduce the topic in a straightforward and accessible way before linking it to cinema. For example you could discuss the region the students live in:

◉ How do they define this area? As a village, town, city, county, region? What characteristics are associated with living in each of these?

◉ Are there any identifiable characteristics such as dialect, food, music etc associated with the region? How many of these can the students recognise?

◉ If students are drawn from a wide catchment area you could explore if they perceive any differences between the places they live.

◉ Is there rivalry with a neighbouring region? What is this based on? What are the characteristics of that region? (These relationships tend to reveal preconceptions of different areas.)

◉ How is the region seen by outsiders? Are there jokes and stereotypes associated with the region? If so, what characteristics do these draw on? Why have they developed? (Students could collect references to their region in national and local news, drama, documentary etc, for analysis of characteristics.)

- How much of the identity of the region is connected to the wider context of its position in the nation? English? Welsh? North? South?
- Has the region ever been portrayed in literature, film or television? If so, consider and discuss these representations.

You could discuss the meaning of national symbols, for example, the flag of St George, which became ubiquitous on cars and in windows, in support of the England football team in Euro 2004 and/or the campaign of the anti-Europe party UKIP in the European elections. At Wimbledon, supporters of the British tennis player, Tim Henman, wave both the Union and St George flags. The newspaper coverage and analysis in June 2004 of these developments would make helpful background reading: see 'The English Identity Crisis', Amelia Hill (20 June 2004) at http://observer.guardian.co.uk.

● National identity and the cinema

Applying the concept of national identity to cinema is complex. One problem in defining what a British film is, is that the term 'British' is often used interchangeably with 'English'. The majority of British films are actually produced in a small but powerful region of England, the South East, making claims that they represent the nation problematic.

Is it useful to define British cinema as comprising a variety of films from Scotland, Wales, England and Ireland? For example, *Trainspotting* (Danny Boyle, 1996), *Sweet 16* (Ken Loach, 2002), *Ratcatcher* (Lynne Ramsay, 1998) are all arguably distinctively Scottish rather than British. *Twin Town* (Kevin Allen, 1997), *House of America* (Marc Evans, 1997), *Yma/Nawr* [*Still: Here/Now*] (Marc Evans, 2003) all proclaim their identity as Welsh films. Irish cinema further complicates definitions, with films from both Northern Ireland and the Republic of Ireland, and with many co-productions with Britain. Shane Meadows' work *24:7* (1997) and *Once Upon a Time in the Midlands* (2002) is securely placed in the English Midlands, so it is also important to consider regional identities.

Students may have a particular preconception of British film, for example seeing them as 'about social problems and everyone is miserable all the time'. Challenge these preconceptions by demonstrating a range of British films. The following worksheet activities illustrate the variety of British films and develop students' independent research and analytical skills.

● Worksheet 1: What is a British film?

The British Academy of Film and TV Arts (BAFTA) has a Best British Film category. The nominations for 2004 were: *Girl with a Pearl Earring* (Peter Webber), *Cold Mountain* (Anthony Minghella), *In This World* (Michael Winterbottom), *Touching the Void* (Kevin MacDonald), *Love, Actually* (Richard Curtis).

In this activity students are asked to research the films on the shortlist to analyse the different ways in which they have been defined as British.

To access worksheets and other online materials go to **www.bfi.org.uk/tfms** and enter User name: **britcin** and Password: **te1511bc**.

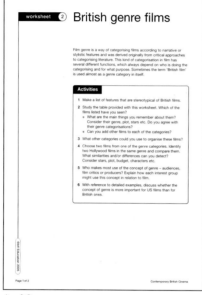

1 of 3 pages

1 of 3 pages

- **Worksheet 2:**
  British genre films

This activity is based on students' own knowledge and experience of British films and introduces a comparison with Hollywood cinema.

Approaches and perspectives used to define British cinema

Definitions and discussions of British cinema usually draw on a range of approaches, which can be identified as follows:

- Representation of national identity
- Film style and aesthetics
- Subject matter
- Cultural diversity
- Legislation
- Funding
- Audience studies
- Influence of Hollywood.

Representation of national identity

It has been argued that British films construct representations of British identity and that central to an ideological reading of these films is the recognition of cultural diversity, devolution and the problem of discussing a single, easily defined concept of Britishness.

Film style and aesthetics

Is it possible to define a film style which is specifically British? There have certainly been distinctive styles of filmmaking at different periods, which have come to characterise British cinema of a particular era. These include:

- Melodrama and historical costume dramas from Gainsborough Studios in the 1940s, eg *Madonna of the Seven Moons* (Arthur Crabtree, 1944), *They Were Sisters* (Arthur Crabtree, 1945), *The Wicked Lady* (Leslie Arliss, 1945);
- Comedies from Ealing Studios in the 1940s and 1950s, eg *Hue and Cry* (Charles Crichton, 1946), *The Ladykillers* (Alexander Mackendrick, 1955), *The Man in the White Suit* (Alexander Mackendrick 1951);
- Horror films from Hammer Productions in the 1950s and 1960s – *The Quatermass Experiment* (Val Guest, 1956), *Dracula* (Terence Fisher, 1957), *The Devil Rides Out* (Terence Fisher, 1967);
- Social realism of the 1960s, eg *Saturday Night and Sunday Morning,* and *A Taste of Honey*;
- Comedy series (or franchises), eg the *Carry On* and *Confessions…* (*… of a Window Cleaner, Driving Instructor* etc) films of the 1960s and 1970s;
- Costume dramas (or heritage/post-heritage films) of the 1980s and early 1990s, eg *Chariots of Fire* (Hugh Hudson, 1981), *A Passage to India* (David Lean, UK/USA, 1984) and *Room with a View (*James Ivory, 1985);
- Gangster movies, eg *The Long Good Friday* (John Mackenzie, 1980), *Get Carter* (Mike Hodges, 1971) and *Essex Boys* (Terry Winsor, 2000);
- *Avant garde*/Art house, eg the films of Derek Jarman, Peter Greenaway and Sally Potter.

Subject matter

The style of British filmmaking is closely linked to the subject matter. One argument for the importance of a national cinema is that it can be culturally specific, eg representing the contemporary life of the country, often through the experiences of groups who are under-represented in more mainstream culture. For example, *Ladybird, Ladybird* (Ken Loach, 1993) follows a single mother's battle with social services to keep her children; *Beautiful Thing* (Hettie MacDonald, 1996) is a coming out and coming-of-age film; *The Full Monty* (Peter Cattaneo, UK/USA, 1997) and *Brassed Off* (Mark Herman, 1996) both explore the effects of unemployment on a group of Northern working class men. *Last Orders* (Fred Schepsi, 2001) compares attitudes to marriage, class and mental illness in contemporary Britain and the 1950s, using a flashback narrative structure.

Cultural diversity

The kinds of subject matter mentioned above are often associated with social realist style and used to define it in an academic context. These discussions take place within a wider debate on the relative value of different cultural forms – the 'great divide' between high art and popular culture. The conventions of literary and theatrical traditions have influenced expectations of national cinema: one associated with middle-class values and tastes. (This could be compared to the French *cinéma du papa* of the 1940s and 1950s attacked by François Truffaut.) This tradition can be seen in recent films including *Howards End* (James Ivory, 1992), *Mrs. Brown* (John Madden, 1997), *Iris* (Richard Eyre, 2002), *Gosford Park* (Robert Altman, UK/USA, 2001), *Sylvia* (Christine Jeffs, 2003). Films which oppose the cultural assumptions and values of this style include *Shaun of the Dead* (Edgar Wright, 2004), *28 Days Later* (Danny Boyle, UK/USA, 2003), *Ali G Indahouse* (Mark Mylod, 2001). These films appeal to a younger, larger audience and draw on American film genres rather than high culture forms. The cultural value attached to these different styles of filmmaking is connected to issues of social class, education and different definitions of art. (For a wider discussion of these ideas, see Strinati, 1995.)

Legislation

Government legislation defines British film in terms of its producers, crew and location. Films Acts have been introduced to regulate quotas and administer tax breaks in the funding of British film. The 1985 Films Act states that a British film must have a producer resident in the European Union, where it must also be shot, and that a minimum of 75% of the wages are also paid in Europe (although this is negotiable when a Hollywood star is involved).

Definitions based on legislation can be very useful in understanding the economic and political contexts of the position of British cinema. For example, the 1927 Films Act was drawn up in response to the dominance of Hollywood, to enforce the quota of British films shown in cinemas, a reminder that competition with the USA has always been a feature of the indigenous film industry. A clause from the same act stated that the scriptwriter had to be British, but this was dropped in 1938.

Funding

Where does the money come from? Does a film have to be made with British money to be defined as British? In terms of legislation 'British' money can come from the European Union and other countries with which Britain has co-production treaties. Some of the most obviously 'British' films of recent years such as *The Full Monty*, *Emma* (Douglas McGrath, USA/UK, 1996), *Nicholas Nickleby* (Douglas McGrath, USA/UK, 2002), *Notting Hill* (Roger Michell, USA/UK, 1999), *About a Boy* (Chris and Paul Weitz, UK/USA, 2002), *Calendar Girls* (Nigel Cole, UK, 2003) were all co-produced with Hollywood companies.

Audience studies

What kinds of films do British audiences watch? There often seems to be a gap between the types of British films studied on academic courses and analysed by critics, and those actually watched by mass audiences. The role of specialist cinemas would be a fruitful area of study, which might consider the increase in screens showing Indian (Bollywood) films, the role of independent cinemas and the programming of 'alternative' films at mainstream cinema chains. The study of the audience at British cinemas is crucial and should not be limited to those watching British films. (See p66 Indian screens.)

How have marketing campaigns used the idea of Britishness to sell movies? Students can refer to their own experiences as filmgoers as well as analysing marketing tools.

Influence of Hollywood

It is impossible to discuss the state of British cinema without also understanding the influence of Hollywood on all aspects of the industry. An audience's expectations about what a film should look like (high budget, special effects, stars), what types of stories they should tell (action, romance, crime), and how they should be released (saturation advertising campaign, widespread exhibition) are all partly created by experience of Hollywood, or dominant cinema. This can make it harder for a low-budget, non-genre British film to find funding or distribution. The role of American companies in distribution and exhibition in Britain needs to be considered and can be linked to issues of globalisation. Multimedia conglomerates such as AOL Time Warner (www.timewarner.com lists all the companies owned by this 'global media and entertainment company') can be used as case studies to discuss these ideas. With Hollywood providing the software (films) and controlling the platforms for exhibition (cinemas, satellite channels, DVD, video etc) globally, what is the effect on national cultures? This relationship is not all one-sided however and the British film industry benefits from investment from Hollywood studios.

It would be interesting to discuss with your students how they, as consumers, view Hollywood cinema. Do they see it as 'foreign' or, in fact, as their own 'home' cinema, with British cinema seeming less familiar? Exploring these ideas, and the ubiquitous nature of American popular culture in the UK, would form a useful icebreaker activity.

How to use this guide

This guide reflects the structure of the student response expected by the awarding bodies. It is very important that theory is integrated through the use of examples (in some cases this might include practical media production work) rather than taught as something separate which students are likely to find difficult and even irrelevant. Throughout the guide students are asked to consider Media and Film Studies debates within the context of British cinema but also within the wider social context, which is crucial to the academic study of film across all specifications. There are suggestions for further work and useful resources which can be used to develop chosen areas in greater depth.

The activities in the worksheets develop students' skills through analysis of film language, representation and ideological readings. Unless otherwise indicated the materials in bold text are available at: **www.bfi.org.uk/tfms**. To access the pages, enter **username: britcin** and **password: te1511bc**. If you have any problems, email: education.resources@bfi.org.uk.

● Schemes of work

Below are two schemes of work. These illustrate the way you could 'pick and mix' from the guide to integrate theory and practice, rather than following the guide from start to finish. These schemes of work refer to worksheets which are available from www.bfi.org.uk/tfms.

Scheme of work 1: Developments in realism

Central to this scheme of work is the definition of realism in British film. It analyses the way that realist styles use particular film conventions, such as social realism, which change over time. The link between film style and representations of particular groups is introduced here in a way that is suitable for AS students but could also be developed for A2 students.

Aims:
On completing this unit, students should be able to:
● Describe the structure and aims of the Film Council
● Recognise the characteristics of social realism in British film at different periods
● Identify the means of construction of the representation of specific groups

Outcomes:
● Comparative analysis of issues of representation in a range of British films
● Critical analysis of the use of different forms of realism

Week 1 Definitions of British cinema
Introduce definitions of and debates around national cinema
Consider subject matter, style, legislation, funding, audience
Students list British films they have seen
Discuss: the UK Film Council – its aims and structure
Worksheets 2 and 3

Week 2 Introduction to realism
Students develop different definitions of realism through textual analysis of extracts, with reference to subject matter and media language
Suggested extracts: *Billy Elliot*, *Bend It Like Beckham*, *Shameless* (Channel 4), *EastEnders* (BBC)
Realism in cinema: Overview of Williams' and Hill's theories (see p38)
Worksheet 6

Week 3 Realism in context: 1960s' cinema and the British New Wave
Historical and cultural context of British New Wave films
Students analyse realist conventions in British New Wave films
Representation of social class: teacher-led discussion placing students' work in the context of representation and audience
Extract: *Typically British* (Stephen Frears) documentary

Or

Week 3 Realism in the 1990s
Comparative analysis of youth culture films (*Trainspotting*, *Twin Town* etc) and social realist comedies (*The Full Monty*, *Brassed Off* etc), exploring the changing conventions of realism (characters, subject matter, film language etc)
Worksheets 7 and 8

Week 4 Realism since the 1990s (1)
Close textual study: *Dirty Pretty Things*
Analysis of the use of genre and social realist subject matter: How effective is this in analysing social problems?
Conventions of the thriller: How do they apply to *Dirty Pretty Things*? **Worksheet 13**
Research the marketing (posters, video and DVD covers, trailers) for the film. How has the genre iconography been used?

Week 5 Realism since the 1990s (2)
Close textual study: *In This World*
Use of documentary techniques in realist filmmaking **Worksheet 17**
Comparative analysis with *Dirty Pretty Things*
  – Different forms of realism used, analysis of film language
  – Analysis of narrative structure
  – What kinds of audience do the films address?
Define both films in terms of belonging to a national cinema

Week 6 Realism and the representation of masculinity
How has the representation of masculinity changed in realist films since the 1960s?
Start with the analysis of Okwe in *Dirty Pretty Things*. Students to produce case studies of the lead male characters from two other films. Case studies to include cultural context, changing gender roles as well as analysis of film language **Worksheets 10 and 11**
How has the role of women in the film affected the representation of masculinity?
Who is the intended audience? How does this affect the representations?
Essay on social realism (See sample questions at www.bfi.org.uk/tfms)

Scheme of work 2: British cinema and representations of national identity

This scheme of work develops a study of representation by linking it to ideological readings of texts. Central to this is the representation of national identity constructed through images of race, culture, religion and place. In the context of the developments in British cinema, this scheme explores how race and the position of refugees/economic migrants have taken the place of social class as 'the subordinate social group'. It is aimed at A2 students who should be familiar with the key concepts.

Aims:
On completing this scheme of work students should be able to:
- Understand the processes of representation
- Define ideology in simple terms
- Analyse the construction of representations of national identity
- Recognise the relationship between producers, text and audience

Outcomes:
- Comparative analysis of representation in different films
- Critical reading of ideological function of representation

Week 1 Introduction to representation and ideology
Review key terms and how representation is used in Media Studies with examples of representations of class, race and gender

Link to ideology: how popular texts (students' own choices) can be read ideologically

Definition of hegemony as dominant and invisible ideology

Worksheet 4

Week 2 Representation of refugees/economic migrants

Discussion of stereotyping, marginalised groups, positive and negative images

Close textual study: *Last Resort* **Worksheets 14 and 15**

Analysis of the representation of refugees/economic migrants and their treatment

Representation of place: what representation of Britain is constructed and how?

How is the audience positioned in the film?

Week 3 Representation of race

Case study: Black British cinema and British Asian cinema

Speaking from within the culture: different characteristics and styles

Influence of Asian culture on 'mainstream' culture

Race and the film industry: comparative analysis of UK and Hollywood texts

Worksheets 19 and 21

Week 4 Representing the nation

Close textual study: *My Son the Fanatic*

Character of Parvez

Use of structural oppositions (conflicts in the narrative) to tell the story

Father's point of view and audience identification

Representation of Britain as a multicultural society, including signifiers of different cultures, segregation, racism

Representation of Bradford

Worksheets 22 and 23

Week 5 The films of Gurinder Chadha

Chadha as auteur: Consider characteristic themes and style in *Bhaji on the Beach*, *What's Cooking?*, *Bride and Prejudice*

Close textual study: *Bend It Like Beckham* **Worksheet 24**

Comparative analysis with *My Son the Fanatic*

Contrasting points of view, sites of conflict

Representation of race, culture, place etc

The representation of gender, particularly women

Different styles of filmmaking

Week 6 Representing the nation (2)
Richard Curtis and Working Title films
Characteristics of Working Title films
Close textual study: *Notting Hill*
Comparative analysis with the representation of Stonehaven in *Last Resort*
Worksheet 25
Essay on national cinema and national identity (See sample questions at www.bfi.org.uk/tfms)

2

Background

What is British cinema for?

Debates about the role of British cinema are not new. Since the increased competition from Hollywood studios from the late 1920s to their current near dominance of UK film distribution and exhibition, the choice for British cinema has always been whether to attempt to compete with Hollywood or to develop a singular, national cinema. Examples of artistic and commercial responses to this situation can be seen in the films of Alexander Korda in the 1930s, Goldcrest in the 1980s (p75 Case study 3) and Working Title now (p78 Case study 3).

The ongoing debates about the aims and purposes of British filmmaking are polarised between two positions:
1. British cinema should be a resolutely national cinema, representing British culture to a British audience. To do this, British films need to be publicly funded.
2. British cinema should be a profitable business, competing in the international marketplace, particularly with Hollywood, by attracting a wide audience.

The chequered history and unpredictable nature of the British film industry and its audiences provides plenty of evidence to support both sides of the argument.

The output of Working Title is often used to illustrate the logic of the second argument. Working Title, responsible for *Notting Hill*, *Bridget Jones's Diary* (Sharon Maguire, 2000) and *About a Boy*, is a financially successful British production company, whose films appeal to the American market as well as the domestic one. The creative personnel involved tend to be drawn from Hollywood and Britain, with female stars such as Julia Roberts and Renée Zellwegger appealing to a US (and UK) mass audience. However, proponents of the first position frequently criticise these kinds of films for imitating Hollywood in their subject matter, their overdependence on stars and genre, their lack of national specificity or investigation of British issues for a British audience.

Support for a cultural cinema and public funding can be found in the work of directors like Ken Loach. In *Sweet 16*, for example, Ken Loach explores the story of a young drug dealer in Glasgow by using local dialect and non-professional actors. This reflects his belief in the importance of representing social issues and groups relevant to the nation first, putting the concerns of attracting a mass audience second. The film would not have been made without public funding. Other established directors such as Mike Leigh, and newer directors such as Lynne Ramsay (*Ratcatcher*, 1998, *Morvern Callar*, 2001), Peter Mullan (*The Magdalene Sisters*, UK/Ireland, 2002) and Gurinder Chadha (see p71) have also benefited from public subsidies. (See the Filmography for a list of relevant films and filmmakers.)

The use of public money for film funding generates particularly heated arguments. The main ways in which the government can distribute funds to the film industry are:

- Direct subsidies such as the use of National Lottery money;
- Indirect subsidies through tax write-offs.

The use of lottery money for certain projects and the establishment of the UK Film Council as a new public body to distribute the funds have proved controversial for a variety of reasons. (See interviews with film director Alex Cox and Chris Chandler of the UK Film Council at www.bfi.org.uk/tfms.)

The role of the UK Film Council

This case study illustrates how debates about national cinema are applied in practice.

The UK Film Council was set up in 2000 to centralise the various means of public support for film, taking over from the Arts Council, which had previously been heavily criticised for the way in which it distributed lottery money to filmmakers. At the same time, it took over the production department of the British Film Institute, arguably a more significant source of subsidy than the Arts Council, funding the first features of many important British directors.

Funding now targets different aspects of the British film industry:

- *Development Fund*: Aims to raise the quality of screenplays produced;
- *Premiere Fund*: Supports bigger budget films and established talent, for example, *Gosford Park*, *Sylvia*, *Young Adam* (David Mackenzie, UK/France, 2003), *Sex Lives of the Potato Men* (Andy Humphries, 2004);
- *New Cinema Fund*: Supports short and feature films; aims to encourage diversity in the industry, for example *The Magdalene Sisters* and *Bloody Sunday* (Paul Greengrass, UK/Ireland, 2001);

- *Regional Investment Fund for England*: Supports nine regional screen agencies (see the interview with Chris Chandler at www.bfi.org.uk/tfms), which promote filmmaking skills, education and understanding of local and regional cinemas.

For further details see the UK Film Council's website: www.ukfilmcouncil.org.uk.

Suggestions for further work

- Get students to research their nearest regional or national screen agency. What educational and training projects is it involved in? Are there opportunities for students to get involved and develop filmmaking skills?
- With the development of digital video technology filmmaking is increasingly affordable. For new filmmakers, the short film provides greater opportunities for production and distribution. For more information on making short films, see: www.ukfilmcouncil.org.uk/shorts and www.animateonline.org.
- Short films can also be used to stimulate discussion on film language, to illustrate the range of new filmmaking, and as case studies for the debates about the role of British cinema. Short films are increasingly available on websites including:
  http://atomfilms.shockwave.com/af/home: short dramas, music videos, animations;
  www.britshorts.com: British and European shorts, industry news.

For more details on short films in the context of British cinema see *Sight and Sound* (May 2004).

Stewart Till is the current chairman of the UK Film Council; he was the deputy chair of the UKFC, Chief Executive of United International Pictures and deputy chair of Skillset. Prior to that he worked for PolyGram Filmed Entertainment and oversaw the international marketing and distribution of successful films such as *Notting Hill*, *Four Weddings and a Funeral* (Mike Newell, 1994), *Bean* (Mel Smith, 1996) and *Sleepers* (Barry Levinson, USA, 1996). He was responsible for acquiring films such as *Trainspotting, The Usual Suspects* (Brian Singer, USA/Germany, 1995) and *Angela's Ashes* (Alan Parker, USA/Ireland, 1999). He is a trustee of the UK National Film and Television School Foundation.

The previous chairman was Alan Parker, a British film director whose Hollywood films include *Fame* (USA, 1980), *Mississippi Burning* (USA, 1988), and *The Life of David Gale* (USA, 2003). His appointment was controversial. Critics argued that it was symbolic of the UK Film Council's bias towards making popular genre films for an international market, rather than the quirky, independent films traditionally associated with British cinema.

John Woodward, the Chief Executive of the UK Film Council has argued that the British film industry has to operate like any other business and consider the best way to make a profit. According to this strategy the UK Film Council should be like a production company or studio, able to compete in the same way as other commercial institutions and should not take unnecessary risks with public money. Woodward has stressed the key areas of style, subject matter, distribution and audience:

> The 80s are behind us. In other words, we do not want to finance social realist art films, nor even Hollywood scale mega productions... The Film Council will help to finance popular films that the British public will go and see in the multiplex on Friday night. Films that entertain people and make them feel good. (Quoted in Pouries, 2000)

This argument has provoked angry responses from a range of film critics, filmmakers and actors, notably Ken Loach, Alex Cox, Ewan McGregor and Tilda Swinton. They argued that this strategy would deny funding to films which did not appeal to the mainstream; the very kind which could not survive without subsidy but which are of artistic and cultural importance. Swinton pointed out that the director Derek Jarman (*Edward II*, 1991 and *Blue*, 1993), with whom she had collaborated, would have been unlikely to receive funding from this Film Council. (Tilda Swinton's speech about the UK Film Council is available at the web journal www.vertigomagazine.co.uk.) Similarly, box office successes such as *The Full Monty*, *East Is East* (Damien O'Donnell, 1998) and *Trainspotting* are used as examples of films with difficult or controversial subject matter (but which were commercially and critically successful), which may not have received funding from the UK Film Council.

Some people believe that British cinema should not receive any public money. They argue that the films funded have been financially (and often critically) disastrous. Before the UK Film Council was established, £100m of lottery money was spent on 200 films, with a total return of only £6m. Often the films failed to find distribution deals and were therefore not even exhibited.

In contrast the UK Film Council has funded films which have often been both commercial and critical successes. The £13m invested in 20 films between 2000 and 2003 generated £125m at the box office, which represents an average return of £9m on every £1m spent. Crucially, successful films repay the funding, providing opportunities for future development. *Bend It Like Beckham* (Gurinder Chadha, 2002) received funding of £950,000 and repaid £1.4m within a year.

Other successful films funded in this period include *Gosford Park*, *The Magdalene Sisters*, *Anita and Me* (Metin Huseyin, 2001), *24 Hour Party People* (Michael Winterbottom, 2001) and *The Importance of Being Earnest* (Oliver Parker, USA/UK, 2002). This group of films feature a combination of established and new directors, British and American personnel and reflect a range of style and subject matter. The films often deal with exactly the difficult themes which critics had argued would be ignored.

In February 2004 the University of Bristol and Watershed organised a conference on British cinema, 'The British Film Debate'. The speakers included the film director, Alex Cox, and Chris Chandler, who both agreed to be interviewed for this guide about their views on the future of British cinema. Chris Chandler, Head of Strategic Partnerships at the UK Film Council, outlined its role in the context of production, distribution and exhibition, and its aim to develop educational and training opportunities for young people. Alex Cox gave his personal opinions about British cinema and funding. Both interviews offer highly contrasting opinions of the current state of British film funding and are excellent material to use with students. They are available at www.bfi.org.uk/tfms.

- ### Worksheet 3: The role of the UK Film Council

Students are asked to explore different debates on funding national cinema through analysis of the work of the UK Film Council and the criticisms made of it. For preparation they should research the aims of the UK Film Council at www.ukfilmcouncil.co.uk and read the interviews with Alex Cox and Chris Chandler.

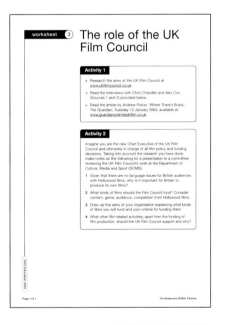

To access worksheets and other online materials go to **www.bfi.org.uk/tfms** and enter User name: **britcin** and Password: **te1511bc**.

Central to Media and Film Studies is the analysis of media texts through key concepts. A grasp of theories of representation and ideology (often referred to in terms such as 'messages and values') are needed to analyse particular social groups, institutions and places in all exam specifications. This guide focuses on the concept of national identity, how a group of films may represent a nation, and the way this intersects with representations of class, race, gender and region.

Representation

The study of representation reveals that media texts are constructions; they re-present the world to the audience. Any media text is mediation, an interpretation of the world. There are several stages of mediation, construction and reception:

- The mediators (editors, producers, directors etc) interpret the 'world';
- This interpretation is informed by the mediator's own background and experiences (class, race, gender, education, age etc);
- The audience receives the interpretation, or representation, through the media of television, news, films, magazines etc;
- Audiences interpret media texts and analyse representations with reference to their own backgrounds, beliefs and experiences.

Meanings created through the interaction of producers, texts and audiences are not endlessly variable; representations rely on the shared recognition of ideas, groups and places. However, there can be disagreement in the interpretation of representations – whether, for example, they are read as negative, positive, inaccurate or partial images – and it is the analysis of how and why these representations are constructed and interpreted that is important.

Richard Dyer (1993) argues that representation is a political tool:

> [How] social groups are treated in cultural representation is part and parcel of how they are treated in life, that poverty, harassment, self-hate and discrimination (in housing, jobs, educational opportunity and so on) are shored up and instituted by representation.

However, Dyer also highlights the complications in theories which focus on the negative representations of class, race and sexuality:

- Are 'negative' representations responsible for the prejudicial treatment of a particular group?
- Does representation directly affect behaviour? See media effects models, such as the hypodermic theory.

- Can 'negative' representations be challenged by 'positive' ones, and change people's attitudes and behaviour?
- Who defines what a 'positive' or 'negative' representation is? Is the representation of Scottishness in *Trainspotting* negative? Is the representation of Englishness in *Four Weddings and a Funeral* positive? Is the racism in *My Son the Fanatic* (Udayan Prasad 1997) (see p69 Case study 2) a negative representation or a form of realism?

Discussion of these points suggests the limitations of studying media texts in isolation. An ideological reading of representations should include the study of society's structures, institutions and power relations.

Ideology

Ideology means a set of ideas, values and beliefs of a particular group, sometimes used to protect the power and position of that group. This concept of ideology was developed by Karl Marx, who analysed the way in which the property-owning class protected their interests by representing the hierarchical class structure, based on ownership of the means of production, as 'natural'.

Ideological processes can be found throughout society in religion, the family, education and the mass media. A popular narrative of Hollywood film is the American Dream: the belief that if you are prepared to work hard there is no bar to success in the United States. Represented as a democratic ideal, this narrative can also be read as an ideological construction; the rich and successful deserve their position while people remain poor because they do not work hard or they lack ambition.

Ideology extends beyond class to other social groups. For example:

- Gender: Patriarchal ideology makes the woman's role as housewife and mother appear natural. In the campaign for gender equality, feminists revealed that this 'natural' role is a construction. Patriarchy is seen as an invisible ideology while feminist ideology is visible.
- Race: The Civil Rights movement of the 1950s and 1960s in the USA and subsequent anti-racist movements have challenged racist ideologies founded on beliefs in the 'natural' and 'God-given' superiority of white people.

Ideologies thus provide a way of explaining the world that represents the particular views of a group who benefit by these ideas, often obscuring or ignoring facts that would undermine their veracity. They appear to justify certain historical realities, such as the social inequality of women or black people, but also help reinforce and perpetuate them.

● Ideology and the media

In the analysis of media representations, it is important to ask whose perspective is privileged and whose is marginalised. The concept of hegemony, developed by Antonio Gramsci, emphasises the way that powerful groups are able to maintain their position through cultural means (particularly the entertainment media), rather than by force. The view that mainstream media are inherently ideological and conservative is found in the work of the Frankfurt School (see Strinati, 1995).

Theorists of the Frankfurt School tended to characterise the audience for popular film as 'cultural dopes', presaging the hypodermic model of media consumption: the mass audience is indoctrinated by the fantasy world on screen, rendering it passive. Cultural, Media and Film Studies question this conception of the audience, arguing instead that the audience plays an essential part in creating meaning and is capable of dissenting from the dominant representation or preferred reading. However, even within these disciplines there are debates about the exact role of the media in maintaining or challenging ideological hegemonies. On the one hand:

● The media endorse the views of the most powerful groups and protect their interests (media owners/producers belong to these groups) through particular representations of social groups, gender, regions, etc;
● The cultural and economic dominance of multimedia conglomerates results in limited space for dissenting views.

On the other hand the media can challenge:

● The dominance of powerful groups by subverting conventional representations;
● The control of multimedia conglomerates by setting up small independent production groups, through the use of new technology.

Agreeing on a definition of what dominant and subversive representations are is increasingly difficult. Does the representation of Okwe in *Dirty Pretty Things* (Stephen Frears, 2002) challenge dominant representations of black males by making him the main character and a sensitive and caring doctor? Or is it so positive as to be an example of misrepresentation? (See p47.) *Sex and the City* (HBO/Channel 4, 1998–2004) has caused a great deal of debate among feminist academics who either celebrate it as a representation of strong, successful women or attack it for its traditional representation of women as obsessed with fashion and men.

The pluralist model is an attack on theories of dominant ideologies. Pluralism argues that the media is a site of great choice and diversity, a stage for competing views and arguments where 'alternative' views are heard.

Examples of this might include the space given to anti-globalisation groups on the news, the positive representation of older women as in *Calendar Girls* (Nigel Cole, 2003) and criticism of America's foreign policy played out in *The West Wing* (HBO/Channel 4, 1999–). This model argues that certain views and representations dominate because they are the most popular, not because they are forced on the masses by a ruling class. It is worth asking how far these examples present significant dissent from dominant ideology. Critics of the pluralist model would suggest it is another feature of capitalist ideology, that, by including criticism of capitalist values, the attack is defused.

- **Worksheet 4: Ideological analysis of advertising**

Students are asked to use textual analysis skills to construct an ideological reading. This approach can be adapted to a range of media texts and is good practice for exams which ask students to analyse an unseen text.

To access worksheets and other online materials go to **www.bfi.org.uk/tfms** and enter User name: **britcin** and Password: **te1511bc**.

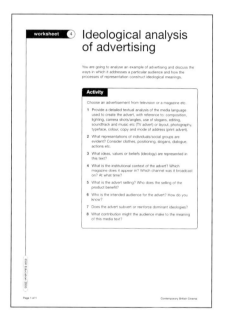

National identity

> It's a moment when the whole nation comes together – like the opening of a Richard Curtis movie... or the manhunt for a serial killer. (Manny in *Black Books*, Channel 4, 2000–)

The concept of national identity should be studied in the context of representation and ideology. The definition of British cinema as a national cinema, ie as representing the nation, raises questions about which nation, and whose nation. Competing definitions of what it means to be British can be read ideologically and it is important to consider the context as well as the content of the representations. The concept of national identity is a construction, a representation based on a particular view of what it means to be British.

Traditional definitions of a nation appeared straightforward. A nation could be defined by a common language, a common religion, borders, territories and a common race.

However, these 'common-sense' categories became increasingly problematic during the 20th century. Can Britain be defined as a nation if:

- People in Britain speak English Welsh, Hindi, Punjabi, Arabic, Gaelic etc? (*Solomon and Gaenor* [Paul Morrison, 2000], a British film in Welsh and Yiddish, won the Oscar in the Foreign Language Film category.)
- The major religions of the world are represented in Britain?
- The British state is composed of four nations – England, Scotland, Wales, Northern Ireland – which, in turn are made up of different regions?
- Britain is a multicultural and multiracial society?

Benedict Anderson (1983) describes a nation as an 'imagined community'. It is impossible for everyone in a nation to know everyone else; instead they share a recognition of certain shared characteristics and values which make their nation distinctive. This 'community' is constructed through literature, language, art and the media. Television plays an important role in 'uniting' the nation. Examples include sporting events (Rugby World Cup, Euro 2004) and Royal occasions such as the Golden Jubilee, where there is a clear assumption of shared national values.

However, increasingly there seem to be no fundamental characteristics which define a particular nation, and an individual's sense of nationality may increasingly be based on particular perspectives or partial views. For example, the debate about Britain's role in Europe sees supporters of both sides of the argument appeal to notions of national identity. For some theorists (eg Paul Gilroy, 1987) any attempt to define a nation promotes nationalism, an inherently racist discourse. The link between racism and nationalism is apparent in the behaviour of football hooligans and in marginal right-wing political parties.

Ideas identifying British cinema as national cinema might have jingoistic associations linked to patriotism and nationalism, but a national cinema can also give voice to marginalised groups.

● British cinema as national cinema

Film plays an important role in providing representations of what it means to be British; this has been particularly clear in wartime with the production of propaganda films. Films such as *In Which We Serve* (David Lean, 1942) reflected the idea of a cohesive national identity, where communities worked together through an understanding and acceptance of their respective positions within the context of nation, region, gender and class, because this cohesion was vital in the face of conflict. This ideological representation works on the shared belief that there is something identifiably British (freedom, determination, the class structure, a sense of fair play) which has to be defended.

Teaching Tip

You could compare the ideas of national identity reflected in these war films with the very different patriotic representations in newspapers during the Gulf War and the Iraq War.

The representation of British identity in wartime has changed in the last 60 years. The films, which emerged in the British New Wave of the early 1960s and the Channel Four Films of the 1980s, reflected an increasingly diverse country in a state of change and instability, which has made it increasingly difficult to discuss British cinema in terms of a nation with clearly defined borders and characteristics. Higson (2000) argues that it is far more useful to think in terms of a cinema of diversity, films which continually question the idea of Britishness and draw attention to its use as a representational form: a post-national rather than national cinema. This argument can be linked to post-modernist conceptions of a traditional, coherent view of national identity disrupted by voices usually at the margins of representation.

● Identity politics

The idea that identity can be defined by nationality reduces something complex to a simple categorisation. The rise of identity politics from the 1960s on suggests that national identity has become less influential than class, race, gender and sexuality. Globalisation, the growth of the European Union and increased mobility all mean that defining nations as distinct and different is more problematic. However, the alternative argument could be made: signifiers of a shared national heritage have greater meaning in a changing world.

Suggestions for further work

Students could keep a diary of their media consumption over a week, making a note of the particular media, genre, subject matter and country of origin. They could then analyse it using the following questions.

1. Is there a link between forms of media and country of origin? (eg, Do you watch American films but British TV programmes?)
2. Does the majority of the media you watch come from Britain or abroad?
3. When you watch films or programmes on satellite TV how do you identify the country of origin?

They may need to research the relevant production companies to answer these questions.

British film abroad

One of the problems (and it is a Catch 22 situation) for the financial survival of a national cinema is that, if it addresses a domestic audience about culturally specific themes, it is likely to find wider distribution difficult. Alex Cox (see interview at www.bfi.org.uk/tfms) argues that a national cinema should also be an international one which has something to say to audiences in other countries. Gurinder Chadha argues that although *Bend It Like Beckham* is set in Hounslow, West London, the themes of the film are universal. As discussed above, the UK film market is dominated by Hollywood cinema and this is also the case, to a greater or lesser extent, throughout Europe. Distribution patterns are likely to dictate whether other countries see British films.

● British cinema and Hollywood

There is a close link between the British film industry and Hollywood:

- British film production companies have co-production and distribution deals with Hollywood studios (eg Goldcrest in the 1980s, Working Title from the 1990s onwards).
- 'British' films can be funded and distributed by US companies, eg *The Full Monty* was financed and distributed very successfully by Fox Searchlight.
- Hollywood studios film in British locations and with British technical crews; inward investment reached a peak in 2003, eg *Harry Potter and the Prisoner of Azhkaban* (Alfonso Cuaron, USA, 2004), *Troy* (Wolfgang Petersen, USA, 2003), *Alfie* (Charles Shyer, UK/USA, 2003).
- Hollywood studios have often used the UK for post-production and special effects techniques.
- British actors work in American films; American stars are used by British producers to widen the appeal of a film.
- British audiences' taste in films is strongly influenced by watching Hollywood films.
- Decisions on which British films to produce and how to market them are often based on the tastes of both domestic *and* American audiences.

There are, of course, British films which succeed in America. This success tends to be linked with the cyclical success of the British film industry, most famously in the 1980s with *Chariots of Fire* and *Gandhi* (Richard Attenborough, 1982). Studying these successes is useful in analysing representations of Britishness. Students could consider:

- What signifiers of Britain are evident in these films?
- Is a coherent image of Britain created?
- Is a particular kind of Britishness favoured by American film audiences?
- What is the ideological reading of these representations?

While the common-sense assumption would be that American audiences have traditionally favoured quaint English heritage films and Hollywood-influenced romances, it is important to consider less immediately obvious successes including *Bend It Like Beckham* (see p71 Case study 2), *The Full Monty*, *Croupier* (Mike Hodges, UK/France, 1998) and *28 Days Later* (Danny Boyle, UK/USA, 2003). For details of the box-office performance of British films in the US, see www.imdb.com, and Gaby Hinsliff, 'Quirky British flicks Crack US Market', *The Observer*, 10 August 2003, available at www.observer.guardian.co.uk.

The definition of a successful British film in America is often relative, but the films of Working Title (see p78 Case study 3) have beaten Hollywood films at the American box office. The first example of this was *Four Weddings and a Funeral*, still the most successful British film in America.

Some pertinent facts about *Four Weddings and a Funeral*:

- It was a co-production between Working Title, owned by PolyGram (a Dutch-owned company at the time), and Channel 4.
- Its budget was $4.3m (£2m); (PolyGram projected a profit between $1.2m and $2.4m).
- It was released first in the US. A British film which failed in the US could still do well domestically, but this is unlikely to work the other way around.
- It was released in Britain with the tagline 'America's smash hit comedy'.

The distribution strategy shows how important marketing is in achieving box-office success. Like most British films, *Four Weddings and a Funeral* was made on a low budget and had only one name which American audiences would recognise. Three different distribution strategies were considered:

- *Wide release*: This means exhibition on approximately 1000 screens across the country, after a limited opening in major cities. This relies on a powerful distributor and is very expensive due to the cost of the number of prints needed and the amount of advertising (P&A). Budget: $11.3m
- *Limited release*: Exhibition on approximately 300 screens, this obviously means reduced cost on P&A, but also limited profit. Budget: $5m
- *Combination release:* The film is released first in major cities (four or five screens); after a week it moves to 20 to 25 screens. If this is successful it is extended to 300 screens then 700 or 800. This innovative approach, now widely copied, enables a distribution company to spend more money when the film is doing well but also to protect its investment if the film performs badly. This was the distribution pattern chosen for *Four Weddings and a Funeral*. Budget: $13m
(Adapted from Kuhn, 2002)

The problems facing British films in the US are clear. Distribution costs can easily be three times the budget of making a film, but without marketing it won't perform at the box office. Students could be asked to consider the challenges of marketing a film in the US, which has a population of over 250 million and hundreds of TV and radio stations, and where the most widely read newspapers are not national but for individual states.

One reason for *Four Weddings'* success was its male star, Hugh Grant. Although the original approach was to market it around the American star, Andie MacDowell, it was Hugh Grant who emerged as the star of the film and he is now arguably the biggest British star in Hollywood. An analysis of the Hugh Grant star persona illustrates how signifiers of Britishness are recognised by British and American audiences.

● **Worksheet 5: Hugh Grant and the construction of a star persona**

This activity provides the framework for analysing the persona of Hugh Grant but could be adapted for use with different stars. It will help students to understand the concepts of representation and ideology.

To access worksheets and other online materials go to **www.bfi.org.uk/tfms** and enter User name: **britcin** and Password: **te1511bc**.

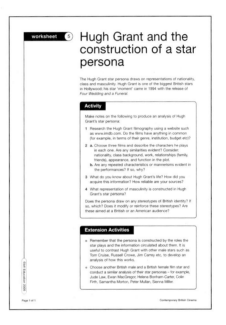

Discussion points

● The constructed nature of a star persona; the roles stars play and the publicity around them;
● Ideological readings of stars (see Dyer, 1999);
● Appearance/mannerisms: things which are immediately identifiable as, for example, Hugh Grant's hairstyle, accent and stuttering delivery of lines.

Suggestions for further work

Students could analyse:
● The tradition of British theatrical stars, such as Judi Dench, Ian McKellan and John Gielgud, working in Hollywood. Their careers and the publicity around them imply a cultural hierarchy in the relationship between English theatre and Hollywood films.

- The role of British characters and the use of British locations in mainstream American films, particularly in action and comedy genres. Analysing representations of national identity by filmmakers of another country allows students to see the way in which the idea operates as a construction. This could be developed through the use of other media texts, eg both the US TV hit sitcoms, *Friends* and *The Simpsons,* produced episodes set in London.

● Britain and European continental cinema

The separation of Britain from Europe, in the context of cinema here, is deliberate.* British film culture has always had more in common with North America than with the rest of Europe, because of the shared language and stylistic similarities between British and Hollywood cinema.

While it is problematic to group together European countries and claim they conform to a coherent film style, Europe, broadly speaking, has long been linked with art cinema, experimentation with form and taboo subject matter. British cinema, in comparison, has (not always fairly) been characterised as less stylistically challenging, emphasising dialogue and realism rather than conspicuous use of film language.

Sorlin (2000) describes some of the factors affecting the exhibition of British films on the continent:

- As in Britain, in continental countries there is competition between domestic and Hollywood films, so there is little room for British films. (Often the market share for British films is as low as two per cent.)
- British films have to be dubbed or (for cinemas in the major cities) subtitled.
- To get British films seen, British distributors promote a small number of 'original, offbeat' films which will get noticed. The distribution and success of *East Is East* in France is a good example.
- British distributors have an advantage over continental distributors in that they are able to promote their films in the US market, which provides extra security.

British films which are popular in Europe provide interesting examples of the way representations of Britishness are understood. Sorlin points to seemingly contradictory representations both of which are popular:

---

* The idea of European cinema is problematic and in the context of British film exhibition, the use of the term 'continental' is more appropriate. However, in Film Studies, the term European cinema is used to signify a style as much as a geographical place.

- Social realism: Films such as *My Beautiful Laundrette* (Stephen Frears, 1985), *Sammy and Rosie Get Laid* (Stephen Frears, 1987), *My Son the Fanatic* (and the New Wave films before them) provided an accessible analysis of the changes in British society. By contrast, continental cinema has often been accused of privileging style over substance and of not engaging with important social issues.
- James Bond: *Octopussy* (John Glenn, 1983) was the biggest British film at the box office on its release and the franchise remains very popular. The Bond character reflects an interesting reading of Britishness too substantial to explore here:

  > ... Bond was seen as the symbol of a United Kingdom that made fun of everything, especially of the sacred values of patriotism and the defence of liberty. (Sorlin, 2000)

Realism and British cinema

● Realism in contexts

Realism is a style which aims to represent the 'real world' honestly and accurately and is central to definitions and discussions of British cinema. It has been influential since the 1930s and includes fiction and documentary film forms.

The notion of British national cinema as a realist cinema, in opposition to Hollywood-influenced films, emerged with the first developments in the realist style, and the critical debates in the 1930s about the preferred style of a national cinema were similar to today's debates. Geoff Brown (1997) discusses how, in the late 1920s, the first serious film criticism in Britain led to the call for a national realist cinema, instead of one which copied American studio models.

> Our railways, our industries, our towns, and our countryside are waiting for incorporation into narrative films. (Paul Rotha,1937, quoted in Brown, 1997)

Mainstream films were produced at Hollywood-style production studios such as Denham, and aimed to appeal to American, as well as British, audiences. They included many costume dramas, such as *The Private Life of Henry VIII* (Alexander Korda, 1933) and *The Four Feathers* (Zoltan Korda, 1939), which connoted a certain type of Britishness, rooted in the past.

● Defining realism in film

Realism is a complex concept because:

- It is used across a range of art forms including theatre, literature, fine art and film, and can mean different things in different contexts; for example, social realism is a specific kind of realism.

- Unlike other art styles, such as Impressionism or surrealism, realism changes over time.
- What appears realistic to one generation may seem exaggerated or melodramatic to later audiences. (Despite this, the use of realism will probably still be recognised by the later audience.)

When applied to film there are further, specific complications because, although film has a particular affinity for realism as the camera is able to capture events as they unfold and often the world created on screen is a believable and recognisable one (settings, costumes, character traits etc), there are the following drawbacks:

- Mainstream cinema, as it has developed, is a genre form, driven by the expectation of glamour, excitement and happy endings, which contradict the concept of realism.
- Film's role as a form of entertainment means that it can be simultaneously defined as realist (it represents the 'real' world to us) and escapist (the world on film is recognisable but better than our own experiences).

In fact, the term 'realist' in film theory is often used to describe Hollywood cinema, despite the tendency of Hollywood films to be fantastic and escapist. Here 'realist' refers to the idea of transparency, the illusion created by narrative, lighting, editing and framing that makes the audience forget that they are watching a film.

It is possible to summarise realism in film as follows:

- It is an attempt to show the world as it is, or at least to convince the viewer that this is what is being represented.
- It is an aesthetic which consists of codes and conventions which the audience recognises as realist.
- While there are characteristics of filmmaking, such as location shooting, naturalistic acting and improvised dialogue, which can often be identified in realist films, these change over time.
- Social realism tends to concentrate on social and political issues, often with a political aim.
- Realism, particularly social realism, tends to be linked to the working class and its preoccupations. This is not because the working class is more 'real' than other groups, but because of its general lack of representation in mainstream film. Hill has suggested that:

  … the idea that realism is linked to the representation of the working class derives in part from context, and specifically the perceived absence of (adequate) representations of this group within the dominant discursive regimes. (Hill, 2000)

Major examples of realist film movements in cinema include: Italian neo-realism, Free Cinema, British New Wave and *cinéma vérité*.

For further discussion of realism, see Armstrong, 2005.

● **Worksheet 6: Defining realism in film and television**

Students will need to watch a range of examples of realist and non-realist texts from film and television, to begin to identify the characteristics of this style.

● Realist texts: a film from the British New Wave, *Brassed Off*, *EastEnders* (BBC), *Coronation Street* (ITV), *The Royle Family* (BBC), *Shameless* (Channel 4), *Life Begins* (ITV). These will indicate some of the different ways that realist techniques can be used for different purposes and audiences. Using TV soaps, and a drama series like *Shameless,* could also introduce a discussion about how television can fulfil a similar role to that of national cinema in representing the nation.

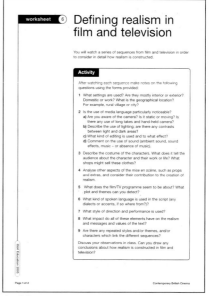

1 of 2 pages

To access worksheets and other online materials go to **www.bfi.org.uk/tfms** and enter User name: **britcin** and Password: **te1511bc**.

● Non-realist text: *The Inspector Lynley Mysteries* (BBC) (or many other police dramas), *Born and Bred* (BBC), *Footballers' Wives* (ITV) and *Bad Girls* (ITV).
● It is also useful to include examples from other countries, such as *Festen* (Thomas Vinterberg, Denmark, 1997) and *La Haine* (Matheiu Kassovitz, France, 1995).
● Examples from US television. *Homicide: Life on the Streets* (USA, HBO) and *NYPD Blue* (USA, MTM), where different techniques are used to suggest realism. See Branston and Stafford (1997).

● **British New Wave**

A brief but influential period of filmmaking in Britain (c 1959–1963), the British New Wave refers to a group of films such as *Room at the Top* (Jack Clayton, 1959), *This Sporting Life* (Lindsay Anderson, 1963) and *Saturday Night and*

Sunday Morning, which rejected the conventions of the Hollywood and home-grown studio-produced films of the time. The New Wave emerged in the context of post-war social and cultural change when people began questioning the role of the ruling class. In politics this could be seen in the opposition to Suez, the founding of the Campaign for Nuclear Disarmament (CND) and the Aldermaston marches. The style developed in these films is referred to as social realism or working-class realism.

Teaching Tip

The British New Wave can also be used to teach other Film and Media Studies specifications. While students can be reluctant to watch 'old, black-and-white films', New Wave cinema seems to be an exception, with students responding easily to the themes and style of the films. There is a lot of useful material available on this period:

- Hewing (2003) provides detailed notes and activities for teachers and students, placing the films in their social and historical context.
- *bfi* Video distribute a range of New Wave films on DVD.
- A key source of study of British cinema in the 1960s is Hill (1986).
- For other resources and a list of key films and characteristics of British New Wave go to www.bfi.org.uk/tfms.

● Form and content

While social realism in cinema is usually associated with politically liberal filmmakers with social consciences, there are arguments over whether realism is a radical form and whether realist films can change dominant representations and make audiences think differently about particular groups or ideas.

Williams (1970) describes how a move towards realism in the arts is usually indicative of a period of social and political upheaval and represents a revolt against the mainstream conventions of a particular art form. For example, the working-class realism of the New Wave was conceived in opposition to middle-class comedies and nostalgic war films. In the 1980s and 1990s, realist films were in part a reaction against costume dramas and upper-class comedies. Williams defines two types of revolt which influenced realism at different periods:

- An injection of new content;
- The invention of new forms.

The British New Wave seems to fit the first type (with an introduction of new types of characters, settings and problems) rather than the second. While there are some experiments in filmmaking such as location shooting and the use of natural lighting, these are still used within conventional film language. European movements, such as *cinéma vérité* or the French New Wave, reflect the second type of realism.

Hill (1986) emphasises how the working-class realism of the New Wave is limited in the way it deals with social issues:

For the social problem film does not really deal with social problems in their social aspects at all (ie as problems of the social structure) so much as problems of the individual (ie his or her personal qualities or attributes).

British New Wave films tend to use elements of traditional narrative such as having:

- A hero for the audience to identify with;
- A series of obstacles for the hero to overcome;
- A narrative resolution – though not necessarily a happy one.

The problems of class are shown from an individual not a collective perspective, implying that the solution to the problems will come from individual motivation. It is worth noting that it is easier to show conditions (of poverty etc) than to explain what produces them, an inherent problem within film realism. According to Hill, the demands of narrative resolution are fulfilled by the hero either opting out of society or adjusting to its demands; the conventions of mainstream narrative do not allow alternative solutions (though many of the films' protagonists fail to achieve their goals or resolve their problems satisfactorily).

To apply Williams' definition of realism, the New Wave did not attempt to challenge how previous films had revealed reality (film language), but challenged what they revealed (representation).

3

Case Studies

Case study 1: Social realism since 1990

The influence of the 1960s British New Wave is still very much in evidence in contemporary British filmmaking, although it is difficult to draw a direct line in terms of style and themes from the 1960s to the 1990s.

● 1960s

In the 1960s, realist filmmaking responded to a period of change in traditional working-class communities. The representation of the working class in New Wave films captured a decline, or perceptions of it, in working-class life, which the films signified through the rise in consumerism, suburbia (such as the dreaded housing estate that Arthur faces at the end of *Saturday Night and Sunday Morning*) and mass culture.

● 1980s

This erosion of 'authentic' working-class culture and politics was central to debates about class and identity in the era of Margaret Thatcher, particularly within the context of the decline of traditional industries, such as engineering, manufacturing and mining. Cinema's response included representations of working-class men as materialist, tasteless consumers, aspiring to become middle class (*High Hopes*, Mike Leigh, 1988). More often though it is preoccupied with the working class as victims of high unemployment and poverty: *Letter to Brezhnev* (Chris Bernard, 1985), *Rita, Sue and Bob Too* (Alan Clarke, 1986) and *Road* (Alan Clarke, 1987).

Hill (2000) identifies the changes which took place in realist filmmaking in the 1980s:

● A shift from class politics to the politics of identity (race, gender, sexuality);
● Fewer images of community and collective action;

- A move away from traditional working-class culture (employment in industry, geographical location);
- Changes in the representation of working-class masculinity (shown as weakened by the decline in work and increased poverty).

● The 1990s: 'Underclass' films and the representation of masculinity in crisis

These changes are evident in the working-class films of the 1990s, particularly the emphasis on personal identity and gender politics. A noticeable change is the rejection of the working-class male as victim. Realist films of the 1990s provided an upbeat narrative about the future of working-class men. The conflict between the reality of economic decline in the north of England and the optimism of a film like *The Full Monty*, suggests again the problems of defining realism.

Monk (2000) refers to the 1990s' films as underclass films. The term 'underclass' has conventionally been used pejoratively by some conservative critics to define a working class which is parasitic and responsible for its own poverty. Monk uses the term neutrally to describe a 'subordinate social class'.

Discussion points

Students could consider:

- Why has Monk decided to use the term underclass? (Why not continue to refer to working-class films?)
- Is it possible to change the meaning and connotations of a word in the way that Monk attempts to?
- Could you suggest a new term to describe these films?

Within the cycle of underclass films, Monk defines two sub-categories: youth culture films and those aimed at an older, 'non-niche mainstream audience'. In both cases the labels apply to the characters in the films as well as the way the films were marketed. These two categories have similarities and differences in subject matter, character and visual style.

Characteristics of 'middle-aged' underclass films

Examples: *The Full Monty* (Peter Cattaneo,1997) and *Brassed Off* (Mark Herman, 1996)

- The underclass is defined as male; female characters are peripheral.
- There is a move away from the context of economic problems to an emphasis on the problems of the male protagonists' loss of confidence.
- Male self-doubt is a result of female equality as much as the decline of traditional industries.

- Women are successful and are resented for usurping the masculine role, but are ultimately supportive.
- The need for men to support other men (fathers and sons, friends, colleagues) is part of the message.
- An entrepreneurial spirit can overcome economic oppression.
- Use of comedy lightens the subject matter.
- The visual style is realist (location, *mise en scène*, costume, dialogue) and transparent ('invisible' film language, little or no stylistic innovations).

Characteristics of the youth culture underclass films

Examples: *Trainspotting* (Danny Boyle, 1996), *Twin Town* (Kevin Allen, 1997) and *Lock, Stock and Two Smoking Barrels* (Guy Ritchie, 1998)

- The representation of membership of a 'subordinate social class' as a lifestyle choice rejects the concept of social problems and solutions.
- The emphasis on a masculine world of dissent (eg drug-taking, criminality) reflects a rejection of mainstream society and values.
- Despite the celebration of dissent, the entrepreneurial spirit (eg from drug-dealing and criminality to becoming an estate agent!) is also celebrated.
- The marketing of the films targets a young, male audience.
- The women symbolise the worlds of work and education, but unlike in the middle-aged underclass films, they are not resented for this.
- The visual style is a mix of realist and anti-realist film language. The anti-realist characteristics include the surreal sequences in *Trainspotting* and the MTV-influenced *Lock, Stock and Two Smoking Barrels*.

Resolutions

Both categories of underclass film provide resolutions, which have been described as fantasy as they rely on a celebration of the individual and his ability to escape poverty through a clever idea (male strippers, a brass band, a drug deal) and tenacity. The problems of economic depression and the end of heavy industry is solved by the free market. In *The Full Monty* a job in the entertainment industry replaces mining. *Brassed Off* is less clearly resolved: there was never going to be a happy ending where the local mine is reopened, but hope is offered in the success of the colliery band. These resolutions may be one of the reasons for the incredible success of *The Full Monty* which provoked a euphoric response in audiences.

- **Worksheets 7 and 8: 'Youth culture' and 'middle culture' realism**
Using the characteristics outlined above, students complete a comparative analysis of different styles of realism, with reference to representations of gender, class and race.

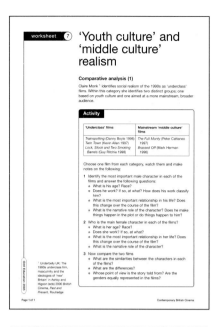

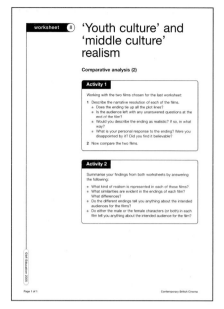

To access worksheets and other online materials go to **www.bfi.org.uk/tfms** and enter User name: **britcin** and Password: **te1511bc**.

Suggestions for further work

You could consider the following

- **Underclass films**:
  24:7 (Shane Meadows, 1997)
  Nil by Mouth (Gary Oldman, 1995)
  Ratcatcher (Lynne Ramsay, 1998)
  Beautiful Thing (Hettie MacDonald, 1996)
  Sweet 16 (Ken Loach, 2002).

- **Youth culture films which focus on female characters**:
  Morvern Callar (Lynne Ramsay, 2001)
  Butterfly Kiss (Michael Winterbottom, 1994).

- **Films, with some 'underclass' characteristics, focusing on middle-class, middle-aged women**:
  Calendar Girls (Nigel Cole, 2003)
  Saving Grace (Nigel Cole, 2000).
  (NB It is important to watch these films in advance to check that the subject matter and treatment is suitable for your particular class.)

- **Ken Loach and social realism**
  Ken Loach is one of the most influential British filmmakers. His films helped to establish social realism in British cinema and to develop it in a politically committed style. Loach's films are ideal for teaching realism and there are many books and resources on his work. An interview with Ken Loach about *Sweet 16* can be found in *Media Magazine*, no 3 (www.englishandmedia.co.uk).

- **Alternatives to realism: British art cinema**
  The focus in studying national cinema is often on the tradition of realism. British cinema also has a tradition of anti-realist, experimental filmmakers including:

  Derek Jarman (*Caravaggio*, 1986 and *Last of England*, 1988),
  Peter Greenaway (*Tulse Luper Suitcases*, 2003, *The Pillow Book*, 1993 and *The Cook, The Thief, His Wife and Her Lover*, 1989),
  Terence Davies (*Distant Voices, Still Lives*, 1988 and *The Long Day Closes*, 1992)
  Andrew Kotting (*Gallivant*, 1997).

Close study films

The three films, *Dirty Pretty Things*, *Last Resort* (Paul Pawlikowski, 2000) and *In This World* were chosen because of their different use of realist subject matter and style.

Discussion points:

- *Dirty Pretty Things* uses a conventional thriller format but realist subject matter.
- *Last Resort* and *In This World* experiment with documentary forms. *In this World*, in particular, blurs the boundaries between documentary and fictional techniques.
- All three films conform to a conception of social realism in constructing new representations of a marginalised, disenfranchised group.
- The films reflect a new cycle of social realism where class is no longer the central concern.
- The representation of refugees or economic migrants is potentially relevant to all Media and Film Studies exam specifications.

Dirty Pretty Things

Dirty Pretty Things deals with the contemporary and controversial issues of illegal immigration, the experience of refugees and the practice of organ smuggling. It places immigrants and refugees at the centre of the film with the story told from their point of view. Consequently, it offers representations of marginalised groups who tend to be either invisible in popular culture or constructed as 'other'.

Similarly, the representation of London in *Dirty Pretty Things* can be read in opposition to those found in films such as *Sliding Doors* (Peter Howitt, UK/USA, 1998) and *Notting Hill*. London is represented through a concentration on interior, often claustrophobic settings, emphasising the restricted, hidden lives of the characters, while the opulence of the hotel lobby where Okwe works is often used as a contrast to the actual homes of the refugees.

The film tells the story of Okwe, a Nigerian doctor living and working illegally in London, who befriends Senay, a Turkish refugee. He uncovers an illegal trade in the internal organs of foreign nationals; a crime made possible by the desperation of illegal workers in the capital. This central plotline functions as a metaphor for the treatment of immigrants in Britain. The identification of the filmmaker with the plight of these immigrants is never in doubt. In interviews, Frears has talked about the way that London relies on an immigrant workforce of cleaners, taxi drivers, porters etc who are never noticed, whose stories are never told. In this respect, Frears' approach is typical of a socially committed, realist filmmaker, such as the directors of Free Cinema and the British New Wave. The point of view of the film is also reinforced by the characterisation of certain groups, such as the immigration officers, as the villains.

Dirty Pretty Things combines social realist subject matter with the thriller genre and uses a *film noir* style. The mix of subject matter, plot and style allows students to analyse different forms and to discuss the link between form and content.

Teaching Tip

Dirty Pretty Things provides a very different representation of the experiences of refugees or economic migrants in London to those found in other parts of the media, particularly in the popular press. The following websites provide some useful contextual information and examples of the way asylum and immigration issues have been represented in the media:

- www.diversity-online.org
- www.refugeecouncil.org.uk/downloads/news/press-myths

Discussion points

- Why was the thriller genre used?
- Does it affect expectations when you know the film is a thriller, rather than 'just' a British film?

Realism and genre

The thriller is a popular genre, sometimes seen as as a subgenre of the crime drama or forming part of a hybrid genre such as the horror thriller, supernatural thriller, psychological thriller, political thriller. You can find a list of thriller conventions at www.bfi.org.uk/tfms.

Hill (1997:1) in discussing *Hidden Agenda* (Ken Loach, 1990) argues that the thriller form is unable to address complex issues because of its genre conventions:

- Genres rely on personalisation through the character of the hero (traditionally, a detective), who the audience is encouraged to identify with.
- This is reinforced by the structure of the detective's investigation and his quest to reveal the 'truth'.
- The detective story formula is inherently conservative as it:
  - depends on the superior powers of the individual and therefore tends to value the characteristics of individualism over the community;
  - relies on the narrative of solving a crime, which encourages identification with the forces of law and order;
  - suggests that good will ultimately triumph over evil (the resolution), even if there are injustices in society;
  - represents corruption or inequalities in society as the fault of unusual individuals (the villain) rather than political and economic structures.

Social realism and Dirty Pretty Things

- **Worksheet 9: Analysis of film language and themes in *Dirty Pretty Things***
Film extract: 0.00–2.10m

This activity could be used as an introductory exercise, before the students watch the whole film, to help guide their viewing. Students can analyse how the opening sequence of *Dirty Pretty Things* introduces its major themes, focusing on the social realist subject matter and the stylised use of film language. You should note that:

- The extract introduces some of the main themes of the film.
- The introduction of Okwe in contrast to the businessmen provides the first of a series of character oppositions.
- Use of film language:
  - handheld, mobile camera, use of close-ups;

To access worksheets and other online materials go to **www.bfi.org.uk/tfms** and enter User name: **britcin** and Password: **te1511bc**.

– use of sound;

– *film noir* style in the use of lighting (in the tunnel and at the taxi office).

● The representation of London through different settings:

– Heathrow airport signifies themes of transience and instability (the film also finishes at the airport);

– The first view of the city is the cab office below a bridge; this panning shot introduces the theme of the legitimate and clandestine worlds of the film.

Representation of refugees

As the hero of the film, Okwe conforms to audience expectations: he is intelligent, resourceful, handsome and strong. Some of the typical characteristics of the hero of the thriller are also evident: he has a secret and tragic past, a capacity for violence which is ultimately tempered by kindness. More unusually for a hero, Okwe is a Nigerian, who is now working illegally in London as a taxi driver and hotel porter. He is also repeatedly shown to be caring and nurturing in ways which are usually associated with female characters.

The representation of Okwe is indicative of the ways in which *Dirty Pretty Things* depicts social issues within a conventional form. The film challenges audience perceptions by having an illegal immigrant as the hero, but this is countered or 'made safe' by other factors: Okwe is a doctor and his reasons for coming to Britain are recognisably legitimate and even heroic.

● **Worksheets 10 and 11: Characterisation of Okwe in *Dirty Pretty Things***

These activities encourage students to analyse how an audience is manipulated to identify with a character and how this identification is used to construct a particular representation. Students should review work stereotypes and the concept of positive and negative images. Analysing the star personas of African-American actors such as Sidney Poitier, Eddie Murphy, Halle Berry and Denzel Washington would be useful in looking at the problems facing black actors in mainstream films.

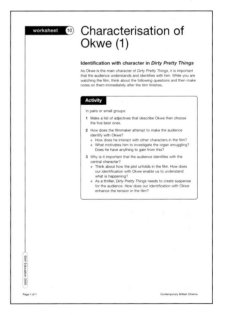

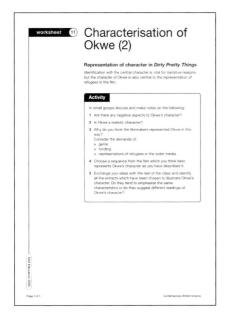

To access worksheets and other online materials go to **www.bfi.org.uk/tfms** and enter User name: **britcin** and Password: **te1511bc**.

● **Worksheet 12:**
Representation of the city –
London in *Dirty Pretty Things*
Film extract: 38.00–41.00m

This sequence follows Okwe as he takes medicine to a man who has been the victim of the organ smugglers. It constructs a variety of images, which show London as a multiethnic city, but one with segregation and extreme poverty. You should note that:

● The representation of refugees goes beyond individual characters to the construction of an alternative London, one which is usually unseen.

● The representation of London is part of the film's comment on the changing identity of the country.

● Through this activity, students should develop their understanding of how *mise en scène* creates meaning.

● **Worksheet 13: *Dirty Pretty Things* and the thriller genre**
Using the characteristics of the thriller (see www.bfi.org.uk/tfms) and close reading of an extract, students can analyse the way *Dirty Pretty Things* uses thriller conventions to tell the story and to create audience identification. Students can compare this film with other thrillers they have seen.

Production context: institutions

Dirty Pretty Things is a co-production from Celador, BBC Films and Miramax, which distributed the film.

Teaching Tip
Ask students to research Celador and Steve Knight.
- Can they find any links between Celador and the BBC?
- What else has Steve Knight, the writer of *Dirty Pretty Things*, written or created?
- How does this affect their expectations of the film?

Discussion points

Students could consider whether
- The BBC should spend licence fee money on film production;
- Funding *Dirty Pretty Things* conformed to the BBC's public service remit;
- There are some types of films which the BBC should not fund.

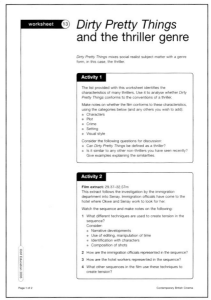

1 of 2 pages

To access worksheets and other online materials go to **www.bfi.org.uk/tfms** and enter User name: **britcin** and Password: **te1511bc**.

The director: Stephen Frears

One characteristic of Stephen Frears' work is the range of genres and subject matter he has covered and his ability to work successfully in the British film industry and Hollywood. Two of his best known films, *My Beautiful Laundrette* (1985) and *Dangerous Liaisons* (1988) illustrate this.

Suggestions for further work

Research films directed by Stephen Frears.
- Which are British? American? Co-productions?
- Are there any similarities in the British films? The American ones?
- Consider genre, subject matter, use of stars and budget. Are any similar to *Dirty Pretty Things*?

Teaching Tip

Stephen Frears participated in a documentary, which marked 100 years of British cinema: *Typically British* (1995, produced and distributed by the *bfi*). This provides a brief history of British cinema and a discussion of different styles of British film, including social realism. The section on this period might suggest some influences behind Frears' own style of filmmaking, and the documentary as a whole makes an excellent, if personal, introduction to the historical contexts of British cinema.

● *Last Resort:* **Themes and style**

Last Resort is a more oblique film than *Dirty Pretty Things*, taking a very different approach to similar themes of alienation and marginalisation. The central character is Tanya, a young Russian woman, who arrives in Britain to be reunited with her fiancé and ends up as a refugee 'by mistake'. With her 12-year-old son, Artiom, she is 'dispersed' to Stonehaven (Margate), where she begins a friendship with Alfie, who, despite being English, also seems to be living in exile; after a childhood of poverty and criminality he has 'escaped' to Stonehaven.

Rather than the highly structured genre form of *Dirty Pretty Things*, *Last Resort* has a looser, more open story. The characters are directionless, their motivations are confused and they make many mistakes. The issues in *Last Resort* are much less clear cut, without the same opposition of good and evil evident in *Dirty Pretty Things*. The structure and film language is also different. There are some linear narrative events but the focus is more on mood and character.

The film language is influenced by documentary techniques such as hand-held cameras, which follow the actor's responses as they unfold, and long takes of the Stonehaven setting, allowing the audience time to scan the frame for details. These techniques and subject matter place it firmly in the realist tradition. However, there are also highly stylised motifs which might be described as surreal within the grey context of Stonehaven: the wallpaper in Tanya's dingy flat, depicting a tropical island; the swirling slow motion of Tanya's blood which of she sells to earn money; the bingo hall where Alfie is the caller.

● **Worksheet 14: Film language in *Last Resort***
Film extract: 0.00–2.38m
The opening sequence provides an excellent example of the different kinds of film language used.

Discussion points

Students could consider:

- The contrast of the use of long, often static, takes in mid- and long shots with the extreme close-ups and continually moving hand-held camerawork;
- The contrast in lighting, eg the green light as Tanya and her son travel through the tunnel in contrast to the white, cold lighting of the immigration checkpoint;

- The use of contrasting styles throughout the film and how film language creates different meanings;
- How Alfie is introduced;
- The use of an airport, a symbol of transient culture, at the beginning and end of the film (as in *Dirty Pretty Things*).

To access worksheets and other online materials go to **www.bfi.org.uk/tfms** and enter User name: **britcin** and Password: **te1511bc**.

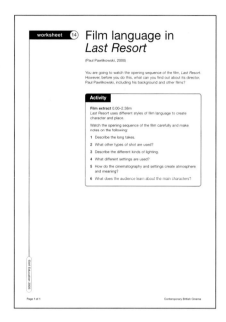

worksheet ⑭ **Film language in *Last Resort***

(Paul Pawlikowski, 2000)

You are going to watch the opening sequence of the film, *Last Resort*. However, before you do this, what can you find out about its director, Paul Pawlikowski, including his background and other films?

Activity

Film extract 0.00–2.38m
Last Resort uses different styles of film language to create character and place.

Watch the opening sequence of the film carefully and make notes on the following:

1 Describe the long takes.
2 What other types of shot are used?
3 Describe the different kinds of lighting.
4 What different settings are used?
5 How do the cinematography and settings create atmosphere and meaning?
6 What does the audience learn about the main characters?

Page 1 of 1   Contemporary British Cinema

The British seaside: Making the familiar strange

Related to the use of film language is the way that, throughout the film, the familiar is made strange because the audience sees it through Tanya's eyes: an Indian take-away, fish and chips ('there's no fish in the fish and chips'), the British seaside itself. When Alfie tells Tanya he is an ex-convict she asks if 'they sent him' to Stonehaven, which seems to her like a prison. This construction of another world, stepped over and unseen by mainstream society, is a major common theme in the two films and could form the basis of a comparative study. In *Last Resort*, Stonehaven is represented as a prison colony, evoking images of concentration camps. Ian Sinclair (2001) comments on this, pointing first to the irony of a Polish-born director representing Britain in a way that is conventionally associated with Eastern-bloc countries:

> Margate is a sanctioned nowhere, a dumping ground for immigrants, runaways and inner-city scroungers. Barter is the favoured form of commercial transaction. Temporary inhabitants, with no stake in society, no voice in civic debate, forget their native languages and struggle with the Esperanto of survivalism. Kids learn English by parroting '10 Benson and Hedges' or 'Fish and chips twice, please.'

- **Worksheet 15: The representation of Stonehaven in *Last Resort***
Film extract: 6.40–9.45m
This clip introduces the audience to Stonehaven as Tanya and Artiom arrive there.

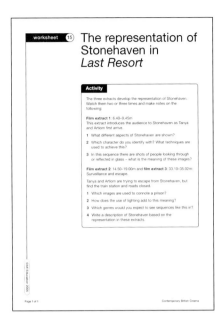

worksheet 15

The representation of Stonehaven in *Last Resort*

Activity

The three extracts develop the representation of Stonehaven. Watch them two or three times and make notes on the following:

Film extract 1: 6.40–9.45m
This extract introduces the audience to Stonehaven as Tanya and Artiom first arrive.

1 What different aspects of Stonehaven are shown?
2 Which character do you identify with? What techniques are used to achieve this?
3 In this sequence there are shots of people looking through or reflected in glass – what is the meaning of these images?

Film extract 2: 14.50–19.00m and **film extract 3:** 33.10–35.02m: Surveillance and escape.

Tanya and Artiom are trying to escape from Stonehaven, but find the train station and roads closed.

1 Which images are used to connote a prison?
2 How does the use of lighting add to this meaning?
3 Which genres would you expect to see sequences like this in?
4 Write a description of Stonehaven based on the representation in these extracts.

Discussion points

Students could consider:

- The contrasting use of long takes, close-ups and hand-held camerawork;
- The use of locations such as the sea front and tower blocks;
- The ways in which the audience is placed with Tanya;
- The image of people looking through, or reflected, in glass (What is the meaning of this motif? Where else does it appear in the film?).

Other useful extracts, which develop the representation of Stonehaven as a prison camp, include sequences at: 14.50–19.00m and 33.10–35.02m.

> To access worksheets and other online materials go to **www.bfi.org.uk/tfms** and enter User name: **britcin** and Password: **te1511bc**.

● Worksheet 16: Realist codes and conventions in *Last Resort*

The representation of the seaside town provides a good opportunity to discuss the idea of realist codes and conventions. The particular shots of the location, Margate (in east Kent), are based on the director's point of view, selected to make a point about the treatment of immigrants. In other words, this is a partial view, constructed for a particular purpose, rather than an objective one. Students could imagine the difference if the shots had been taken in sunshine, for example. This socially committed, political analysis of Tanya's story places Pawlikowski's work in the tradition of British social realism. This activity shows students how meaning

worksheet 16

Realist codes and conventions in *Last Resort*

The representation of the British seaside town in *Last Resort* is created through the selection of particular shots of Margate; this constructs a specific idea about the town for the audience. In this activity you are asked to consider the way that choices about locations, composition, type of shots used and lighting can create different meanings.

Activity

Work in pairs or small groups:

You work for a production company which has been commissioned by the local tourist board to do a short promotional film about your town:

- Choose between four and six settings that you think show your town in a positive way, outlining the reasons for your choice.
- Storyboard a sequence of approximately 12–18 shots in which the location is introduced to the audience. This may be from the point of view of a particular character. The aim of your sequence is to make the audience understand that this is a positive representation.
- Produce a script which details camera movement, cuts, lighting and any dialogue.

Individually:

- Write a short analysis (approx 400 words) of your storyboard and script explaining the reasons for your choices.

is created through selection and construction and gives them practice in storyboarding.

Suggestions for further work
Characterisation and imagery
Film extract: 48.28–50.01m

This extract stands out in the film as a moment of happiness for the characters. Tanya, Artiom and Alfie are shown enjoying the seaside, which functions in a similar way to the use of the countryside in the New Wave films. Also look at the use of imagery and sound. Students could analyse the way these elements of film language are used to create meaning. The concept of text (Tanya, Alfie and Artiom enjoy their time together at the beach) and subtext (they long for escape and their happiness here is only fleeting) could also be discussed.

Comparative text: The British film *Last Orders* (Fred Schepisi, 2001) represents Margate in a very different way indeed and would make a good comparison in analysing images of regional identity.

● *In This World*: Realism and the docudrama

In This World follows two refugees, Jamal and Enayat, as they travel from Pakistan through Iran, Turkey and Italy, to Dover and finally London. The journey is filmed using small digital video cameras, improvisation, available light and non-actors. Students are likely to find *In This World* the most difficult of the three films because of its documentary techniques, minimal dialogue and lack of characterisation. It is important therefore to provide a context and introduction to the film to help students engage with it. Analysing the opening sequence as a separate exercise before showing the film and stopping the film to discuss what is happening during the screening should help. If students have done Worksheet 1: What is British film?, they will already be familiar with the story and production context. As *In this World* is a docudrama it would also help if students discussed documentary techniques.

Comparative texts

The docudrama is a popular form on British TV and includes films made for television such as *The Navigators* (Channel 4, Ken Loach, 2001), *Out of Control* (BBC1, Dominic Savage, 2002) and *Bloody Sunday* (ITV1, Paul Greengrass, 2001), which all had cinema releases. The docudrama form is controversial precisely because it dramatises actual events. Critics argue that the need for drama leads to compromises in the truthful retelling of events.

In this World takes docudrama to an extreme because it follows a real boy on a real journey and it is hard to distinguish between fact and fiction. The central characters, Jamal and Enayat were refugees planning their escape from a camp in Pakistan to travel to London. The credits state: Jamal Udin Torabi:

Himself; Enayatullah: Himself – the boys are 'playing' themselves. When filming ended in London, Jamal applied for political asylum. The choice of what to film also combines the techniques of documentary and fiction filmmaking. Shots were taken without the knowledge of the people in them, but other scenes were set up in advance with the use of actors. Most of the dialogue is improvised, but based on a script by Tony Grisoni, who interviewed others who had made the journey.

- **Worksheet 17: Documentary techniques in *In This World***

Film extract: 0.00–3.45m

This sequence illustrates the use of conventions from documentary form and the activity helps students to distinguish between different characteristics of film language.

Discussion points

Students could consider:

- The film's opening: a voiceover gives information about the Afghan refugees at the camp in Pakistan, stating that they left Afghanistan after the Soviet invasion in 1979 and the US bombing in 2001. It gives an historical context to the story and also suggests the point of view of the filmmaker.
- The use of hand-held digital cameras and the grainy look of the film.

To access worksheets and other online materials go to **www.bfi.org.uk/tfms** and enter User name: **britcin** and Password: **te1511bc**.

- **Worksheet 18: Film language and identification with characters in *In This World***

Film extracts: 48.50–51.27m and 59.35–1h.04m

These two extracts are examples of the way the film language changes during the film. As the film progresses, the documentary convention of voiceover disappears and we follow the journey itself. It is useful to compare *In This World* to a mainstream, scripted drama. There the dialogue would be used to reveal aspects of character, and the journey might be more like a road movie where lessons are learned and friendships formed. Instead there is very little dialogue to explain what is happening and the use of real-time filming recreates the experience of the long hard trail. This and the experimental use of film language places the audience with the refugees – scared and not knowing what will happen to them.

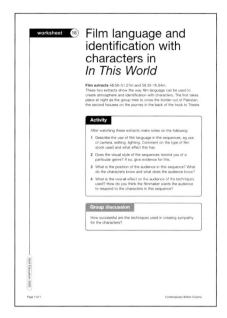

worksheet 18 Film language and identification with characters in In This World

Film extracts 48.50–51.27m and 59.35–1h.04m.
These two extracts show the way film language can be used to create atmosphere and identification with characters. The first takes place at night as the group tries to cross the border out of Pakistan; the second focuses on the journey in the back of the truck to Trieste.

Activity

After watching these extracts make notes on the following:

1 Describe the use of film language in the sequences, eg use of camera, editing, lighting. Comment on the type of film stock used and what effect this has.

2 Does the visual style of the sequences remind you of a particular genre? If so, give evidence for this.

3 What is the position of the audience in this sequence? What do the characters know and what does the audience know?

4 What is the overall effect on the audience of the techniques used? How do you think the filmmaker wants the audience to respond to the characters in this sequence?

Group discussion

How successful are the techniques used in creating sympathy for the characters?

Page 1 of 1   Contemporary British Cinema

To access worksheets and other online materials go to **www.bfi.org.uk/tfms** and enter User name: **britcin** and Password: **te1511bc**.

Discussion points

The first extract takes place at night as the group tries to cross the border out of Pakistan, the fields are covered in snow, a patrol nearby shoots at them and the air of fear and panic is palpable. Students could consider:

- The way the film language creates atmosphere, eg the use of hand-held cameras, 'night vision' filming;
- How the film style borrows from horror conventions;
- The audience's restricted view. We can only see what the refugees can see. With the exception of the voiceover in the first part of the film, *In This World* is told in restricted rather than omniscient narration;
- Which of the sequences are 'real' and which are staged? According to some critics, the gunfire at the border seem real.

The second extract uses similar techniques to capture the horror of the journey in the back of the truck which takes them to Trieste. Again, the use of darkness and sound effects are vital to communicating the experience.

Dirty Pretty Things and *Last Resort* (and another British film about immigrants, *Beautiful People*, Jasmin Dizdar, 1999) focus on the experience of refugees in Britain, while *In This World* finishes as Jamal arrives in Kilburn. There are no easy solutions offered. This may be one of the reasons that *In This World* did not do well at the box office, despite excellent reviews. The openness of the ending, as with *Last Resort*, links *In This World* to an alternative form of cinema which rejects mainstream conventions such as genre and neat endings.

Suggestions for further work:
'Alternative' endings
Film extract: 1.18.50–1.22.46m (including the beginning of the end credits)

This shows Jamal's arrival in London at his friend's restaurant. The sequence cuts between Jamal praying in a mosque and the children in the camps in Pakistan. Students could consider:

- The use of cross-cutting to compare the two countries and cultures and to underline the meaning of the title of the film – they are all 'in this world' – through an interconnection of countries, races, religions which it is impossible to draw borders between;
- The different signifiers of the two cultures and the way in which they have become mixed, eg the shot of the interior of the mosque.

Case study 2: British Asian cinema

A characteristic of British cinema in the 1990s has been the emergence of British Asian (or Anglo-Asian) cinema. The term refers to films which examine the position of Asian communities in Britain, often focusing on the complex experiences of second generation British Asians growing up within both cultures. Within the context of a national cinema, the definition of British Asian cinema raises interesting debates:

- Are British Asian films part of, or outside, national cinema?
- What is the relationship of British Asian cinema to black British cinema?
- How do the opportunities for production, distribution and exhibition of British Asian films affect the nature of those films?

While many Asian filmmakers would not identify themselves as black, British Asian cinema has conventionally been discussed as part of black British cinema as these films are often seen as challenging traditional non-white representations. Stafford (2001) claims that this is partly due to the way that the industry views both Asian and black films as being outside the mainstream. This definition of mainstream includes Hollywood but also 'white' British cinema. The increasing use of the term British Asian cinema suggests the positive development that British films of Asian experiences, made by British Asians, are now more visible and popular. However, it is also the case that, after a commercial breakthrough in the 1980s and 1990s, the opportunities for black British filmmakers, referring to African and Caribbean communities in the UK, have declined.

● Black British cinema

Key films:

Pressure (Horace Ove, 1975)
Handsworth Songs (John Akomfrah, 1986)
Playing Away (Horace Ove, 1986)
Looking for Langston (Isaac Julien, 1988)
Young Soul Rebels (Isaac Julien, 1991)
Seven Songs for Malcom X (John Akomfrah, 1993)
Speak Like a Child (John Akomfrah, 1998)

Historical overview

Black British cinema specifically refers to a group of films produced in the mid-1980s and early 1990s, which took a number of forms, from mainstream narrative feature films such as *Playing Away* to experimental documentaries such as *Handsworth Songs*.

One of the government responses to the civil disturbances of the late 1970s and 1980s was to fund local black cultural projects, in recognition of the fact that black artists had been excluded from mainstream cultural practices including cinema and the fine arts. At the same time, in 1982, Channel 4 was set up, with the remit to address 'minority' groups, and co-funded many black feature films and documentaries.

One striking feature of this period is the way that black British filmmakers challenged not just representations but also mainstream film language and production, based on the belief that questioning dominant views (such as the representation of race or a particular political system) required the use of new forms. In European filmmaking of the 1960s, this was referred to as counter-cinema. Co-operatives such as the Black Audio Film Collective and Sankofa were set up to produce films collectively in a rejection of the hierarchical system of studios where the producers and financiers make decisions.

In turn, the style of the films was often different from mainstream productions, using experimental narrative forms and film language to discuss black identity in Britain. (For an accessible discussion of co-operative filmmaking, see Branston and Stafford, 1997). For example, *Handsworth Songs*, produced by the Black Audio Film Collective was a controversial but influential documentary about the Handsworth riots in Birmingham in 1985 and how they were represented in the media. Rather than follow the documentary tradition of presenting 'a window on the world', *Handsworth Songs* uses archive film, still images, news reports and sounds from the period, as well as original material. There is no narrator to explain the film and the audience is expected to analyse and interpret the images for themselves.

In contrast, *Playing Away* is a mainstream feature film, written by Caryl Phillips, which offers an alternative approach to analysing racism and the black experience in Britain. The comic premise of the film (a South London cricket team of West Indian immigrants is invited to a traditional English village to play a cricket match) is expressed through conventional film forms of narrative and identification. The narrative is structured around cultural (race and region) differences to entertain, and hopefully enlighten, a mass audience. More recently, *Wondrous Oblivion* (Paul Morrison, UK/Germany, 2003) takes a different approach to a similar subject, telling the story of a white English boy in the 1970s who is inspired to play cricket by the arrival of West Indian neighbours.

Discussion points

- The aim of the Black Audio Film Collective was to get audiences to think differently about issues by presenting them in new ways. This raises questions about what we expect from film which could be explored with students:
    - Should film provide escapist entertainment or can it be used for political purposes? Why do we go to the cinema?
- Black British films feature both a range of styles and subject matter as well as shared characteristics:
    - The filmmakers speak from within ethnic groups, rather than for them. They have a 'voice'.
    - There is an emphasis on representing the heterogeneity of cultures.
    - Members of different cultures are shown as complex individuals, not just as victims.
- Paul Willemen (1989) discusses black British filmmakers as being both 'Other' but also part of British culture; they inhabit an 'in between' position or third space:
    - Do these characteristics apply to other groups of (British) films?
    - What is the difference between speaking from within a particular group and speaking for it?
    - Are there groups in this country who are still spoken *for* in film and the wider media?

Black British cinema now

Recent writing on black British cinema has been marked by pessimism about the opportunities for funding, distribution and exhibition, which have declined in the 1990s. Pines (1997) writes:

> … the 1990s have seen the emergence of a completely new cultural and political agenda in Britain, which has temporarily halted any new interventions in the area of black representation. This does not bode well for the immediate future.

This changing cultural and political agenda is also highlighted by Alexander (2000). Asking why the breakthroughs made by black directors in previous decades have not been developed, she argues that it is partly due to the shift in thinking about national cinema – away from cultural goals to commercial ones.

> Although there is a renaissance in British cinema, backed by millions of pounds of Lottery money, the Britain that is being disseminated on the screen and around the world is steeped in heritage, literary culture and conventional ideas of class relations. It is also overwhelmingly white, in sharp contrast to our workplaces, high streets and bedrooms, which tell a very different story… It is a narrow and nostalgic view of Britain which is presented.

● **Worksheet 19:**
Representations of black and Asian characters

This activity draws on students' own film viewing and asks them to analyse the representations of race in recent British and American cinema.

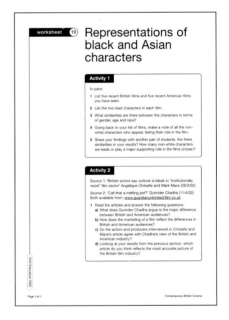

> To access worksheets and other online materials go to **www.bfi.org.uk/tfms** and enter User name: **britcin** and Password: **te1511bc**.

● **British Asian cinema**

Key films:

My Beautiful Laundrette (Stephen Frears, 1985*)*
Brothers in Trouble (Udayan Prasad, 1996*)*
My Son the Fanatic (Udayan Prasad, 1997)
East Is East (Damien O'Donnell, 1998)
Bhaji on the Beach (Gurinder Chadha, 1995)
Bend It Like Beckham (Gurinder Chadha, 2002)
Anita and Me (Metin Huseyin, 2002)
Bride and Prejudice (Gurinder Chadha, 2004)

All these films, written or directed by British Asians, exemplify how British Asian identity is constructed through the demands of conforming to or rejecting Western (often American as well as British) and Asian cultures. This conflict is dramatised through a range of social and cultural practices: religion, 'arranged' marriages, generational conflict, gender expectations, sexuality and racism. The majority of the films take the point of view of the second- (or third-) generation characters, for instance, the children of parents who came to Britain in the 1960s and 1970s. Exceptions to this include *Brothers in Trouble* and *My Son the Fanatic*, which tell their stories from the father's point of view. *My Beautiful Laundrette* explores the problems of integration for first-generation immigrants as a secondary narrative.

Discussion points

Students could consider:

- What effect it has when the younger (or older) generation is central to the story;
- How stories would be affected if more films were from the point of view of first-generation immigrants;
- Reasons for the focus on second- and third-generation immigrants. (Who are the filmmakers and the audience? What problems are there in raising money?)

● Production, distribution and exhibition

All the above films were funded or part-funded by public service broadcasters (BBC, FilmFour, Channel 4) and public money (Arts Council, UK Film Council). *My Beautiful Laundrette*, *East Is East* and *Bend It Like Beckham* were critical and commercial successes in the UK and America. *Bend It Like Beckham* is the highest grossing, purely British-funded film to date. But *Anita and Me* did poorly at the box office, despite being based on Meera Syal's best-selling novel.

Budget and box-office revenue

Film	Budget (£m)	UK BO (£m)	US BO($m)
Bhaji on the Beach	1.00	0.310	N/R
Bend It Like Beckham	2.70	11.552	32.5
East Is East	2.40	10.375	4.2
Anita and Me	2.90	1.851	N/R

For comparison here are the details for three mainstream British films, produced by commercial companies in a similar period:

Film	Budget (£m)	UK BO (£m)	US BO ($m)
Kevin and Perry Go Large (Ed Bye, 1999)	4.00	10.461	N/R
Bean (Mel Smith, 1996)	16.20	17.973	45.3
Ali G Indahouse (Mark Mylod, 2001)	4.00	10.297	N/R

UK figures from Wickham (2003), US figures from www.imdb.co.uk
BO: Box office; N/R: not released

Although *Bean* is the highest-grossing film, its comparatively high budget (for a British film), when compared to *Bend It Like Beckham*, means it was much less profitable. The British films which were not released in America also provide an interesting point of discussion. Why did *East Is East* gain distribution but not *Kevin and Perry Go Large*?

The following table shows the highest number of screens each film achieved during release in the UK and US:

Film	UK	US
Bend It Like Beckham	384	1002
East Is East	256	157
Anita and Me	226	N/R
Kevin and Perry Go Large	365	N/R
Ali G Indahouse	396	N/R
Bean	345	1948

The number of screens indicates what kind of success the distributors and exhibitors predicted for each film and puts the box-office gross figures into context. The number of screens in the US in comparison to the UK is also helpful in understanding the importance (or otherwise) of the UK to the Hollywood film industry. These figures are available for current films in the Review section of *The Guardian* (Fridays).

- ## Worksheet 20: Budget and box office

This activity requires students to analyse the reasons for films' relative success and failure at the box office.

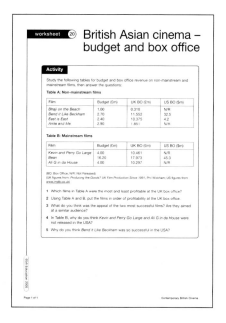

To access worksheets and other online materials go to **www.bfi.org.uk/tfms** and enter User name: **britcin** and Password: **te1511bc**.

- # Bollywood-influenced British films

Bollywood Queen (Jeremy Wooding, 2002) and *The Guru* (Scherler Mayer, UK/France/USA, 2002) are evidence of the fashion for Bollywood and the importance of young British Asian consumers to the film industry. These are mainstream films which take aspects of Bollywood film style and Indian culture, particularly fashion and music, and integrate them with mainstream genre forms. Also see the *bfi*'s specialist website: www.imaginasia.org.uk.

This trend has extended beyond film. The summer of 2002 was dubbed 'Indian Summer' in response to the opening of the musical *Bombay Dreams* in London, the screening of a season of Indian films on Channel 4, and the fact that Selfridges (London) had a 'Bollywood' make-over. Recent examples of this cultural 'borrowing' include a Channel 4 reality style show, *Bollywood Star*, the use of Indian dancers in the BBC1 idents and in adverts selling beer, cars and building societies. The novels *White Teeth* by Zadie Smith and *Brick Lane* by Monica Ali have been both bestsellers and critical successes.

- ## Worksheet 21: Representations of Asian culture in British media

This activity asks students to do some independent research into the representation of Asian culture in the mainstream media and to prepare a class presentation.

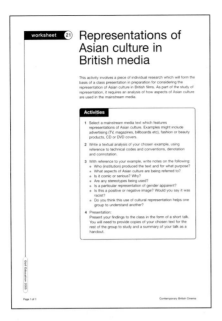

● Indian screens

The increasing popularity of Indian films is evident in the mainstream exhibition of 'Bollywood' films. Cinemas in London, Leicester and Birmingham, particularly, show films such as *Lagaan* (Ashutosh Gowariker, India, 2001), *Kuch Kuch Hota Hoi* (Karan Johar, India, 1998), *Dev* (Govind Nihalani, India, 2004), which have all been in the UK box-office top 10. *Dev* was released on 11 June 2004 on 25 screens, with an opening weekend gross of £40,509, which put it at number 10 (*Troy* was on 413 screens and took £720,745, putting it at number 3).

Star City, a purpose-built cinema complex of screens, restaurants, bars and a megabowl, opened in Birmingham in 2000. Of the 21 screens, four are dedicated to showing Bollywood films. For further details see: 'Bombay Breakout', Jessica Winter, *The Guardian*, 12 December 2003.

Suggestions for further work

Get students to produce a list of all the local exhibition spaces.

- How many screens are there?
- What kinds of films are shown?
- Does the local cinema show any alternatives to mainstream film?
- If so, what kinds and how are these films promoted?

● International Indian films

The link between British and Indian filmmaking is also noticeable in the development of Indian films, often with British producers or directors, which have been released simultaneously in India, the UK and North America. For example:

Salaam Bombay (Mira Nair, India, 1988)
Kama Sutra (Mira Nair, India, 1996)
Monsoon Wedding (Mira Nair, India/USA/France/Italy, 2001)
Bandit Queen (Shekhar Kapur, India/UK, 1994)
The Warrior (Asif Kapadia, UK/France, 2001)

These films had a similar distribution and exhibition pattern in Britain to European art-house cinema, appealing to a similar niche audience, who are likely to be older and middle class.

● Rethinking national cinema

The emergence of British Asian cinema in the 1990s suggests that ideas about what it means to be British, and how this identity is represented, are changing. In addition to providing new representations of particular groups, these films encourage people to question the concept of national cinema:

> It is difficult to define cultural diversity and cultural specificity in solely national terms, it is more helpful to consider 'local' or 'transnational' contexts. (Higson, 2000)

The films referred to as British Asian tend to be firmly rooted in regional locations: West Yorkshire (*Brothers in Trouble*, *My Son the Fanatic)*, Birmingham and Blackpool (*Anita and Me*, *Bhaji on the Beach*) and Salford (*East Is East*). When the setting is London, it concentrates on the outskirts and suburbs such as Hounslow (*Bend It Like Beckham*) rather than the more cinematically familiar West End. In their choice of northern locations, British Asian films can be linked to the New Wave.

There is a transnational character to many of the films. While the physical settings are in Britain, the countries of origin of the Asian characters also exert a strong influence. These tend to be used either as a symbol of a more authentic and spiritual way of life, which the older generation are fearful of losing, or as a representation for the younger characters of tradition and restriction. References to Asian culture often create comic moments by highlighting and exaggerating (generally non-controversial) cultural differences, such as the children secretly cooking bacon in *East Is East* or Jesminder's mother's fruitless attempts to teach her daughter to make *aloo gobi* in *Bend It Like Beckham*.

Increasingly, 'British' as a brand incorporates transnational features which help to sell films abroad. Traditionally, the concept of Britishness signified heritage films, costume dramas and literary adaptations. With the success abroad of films like *East Is East* and *Bend It Like Beckham*, other kinds of British cinema are being recognised. Thus we could say:

- Nations are diasporic, 'forged between unity and disunity' (Higson, 2000)
- National cultures increasingly include productions from the perspective of disenfranchised minorities.

Recent writing on national cinema argues that a paradox is inherent in the concept. Traditionally, a national cinema has been defined by a sense of common identity and continuity, an understanding of what a particular nation is and represents. It is represented as different from other national cinemas. However, Hayward (2000) argues that co-existing with differences has become a reality and is at cross-purposes with the idea of the nation as a unified identity, thus undermining the idea of a national cinema in this sense.

Comparative text

The Channel 4 series *White Teeth* (2003), an adaptation of the novel, tells the story of Asian immigrants in London from the 1950s to the present day. The central characters are long-standing best friends from different cultures and the series explores the ways in which British and Indian history and politics are intertwined.

● *My Son the Fanatic* and *Bend It Like Beckham*

My Son the Fanatic and *Bend It Like Beckham* provide many points for comparative analysis. They are both accessible, and in the case of *Bend It Like Beckham* familiar, films which students should respond well to. The main area of comparison is the contrasting points of view used. As the title suggests, *My Son the Fanatic* is a father's story, while *Bend It Like Beckham* focuses on the experiences of a daughter.

There is also a different emphasis in the style and subject matter of each film. While *My Son the Fanatic* has humorous moments, the tone is much more sombre than that of *Bend It Like Beckham,* which is closer to the British social realist comedies of the late 1990s. This difference in tone is evident in the way that the films explore the responses of the characters to different interpretations of British and Asian culture. The optimism of the representation of an integrated society in *Bend It Like Beckham* contrasts with the view of increased segregated fundamentalism in *My Son the Fanatic*. Another noticeable difference is the level of success achieved by each film: *My Son the Fanatic* received limited distribution despite good reviews while *Bend It Like Beckham* was a great commercial success. Students should be encouraged to think about the reasons for this.

● *My Son the Fanatic*: Major themes

My Son the Fanatic explores the disappointments and doubts of a British Asian man, Parvez, who works as a taxi driver in Bradford. The film constructs Parvez as proud of his city, rooted in its culture and people. He is a humanist rather than a man shaped by religious beliefs. This allows him to form a strong friendship with Bettina, a prostitute.

One of the film's most interesting aspects is the way in which Parvez's position as an immigrant and Bettina's work as a prostitute are linked; they are both seen as outsiders, exploited by more powerful people. Parvez's life is also compared to that of Mr Schitz, a German businessman who is converting an old mill into a supermarket. The major conflict centres around the son Farid, who rejects the culture he has been born into, and therefore his father, to follow fundamentalist religious teachings. 'Our cultures cannot be mixed', says Farid. 'Everything is already blending', replies his father. *My Son the Fanatic* reverses the norms of generational conflict in British Asian cinema by making the son the one who rejects 'Western' values and the father the one arguing for greater integration.

● Worksheet 22: Narrative and conflict – the representation of British and Asian culture

Students are asked to consider how arguments over identity create the conflicts which shape the narrative, then examine two film extracts.
Film extracts: 22.00–26.07m and 46.25–51.11m

The first extract focuses on the increased estrangement between Farid and Parvez due to cultural differences. This extract positions the audience with Parvez and reveals his growing loneliness and isolation. The second extract illustrates the way in which the film constructs the representations of cultures through characterisation, dialogue and *mise en scène*.

1 of 2 pages

To access worksheets and other online materials go to **www.bfi.org.uk/tfms** and enter User name: **britcin** and Password: **te1511bc**.

Discussion points

Students could consider:

- The use of oppositions to structure narrative, creating dramatic conflict and identification with characters;
- The bond between Parvez and Bettina and the tension between Parvez and Minook;
- The opposing views on life that Farid and Parvez hold and how these reflect different cultural values;
- The representation of women, seen as objects and inferior by all cultures.

Points to note

- Throughout the film and specifically in the second extract, the composition of shots to provide information on the characters;
- The use of different settings – the home, the restaurant, the nightclub – to signify the relationships between characters;
- The use of settings, props and costumes signify British and Asian culture and the 'muddle' of these cultures;
- The use of soundtrack in creating meaning.

- **Worksheet 23: Resolution in *My Son the Fanatic***
Film extract: 1h18.21–1h23.00m (the final minutes of the film including some of the credits)

Discussion points

Students could consider:

- The resolution – or lack of resolution – of the different conflicts in the film;
- The use of a more open ending, where the audience is left with questions about what happens to the characters;
- The symbolic use of settings, for instance, the woods in which Bettina and Parvez meet, the empty house;
- The use of music.

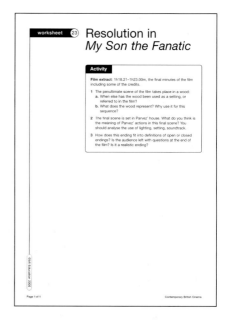

To access worksheets and other online materials go to **www.bfi.org.uk/tfms** and enter User name: **britcin** and Password: **te1511bc**.

● Gurinder Chadha and Bend It Like Beckham

Chadha's feature films, *Bhaji on the Beach*, *What's Cooking?* (USA, 2000), *Bend It Like Beckham* and *Bride and Prejudice*, make her the most successful contemporary British female director. The difference in the promotion and reception of her first feature and the most recent ones, is indicative of some of the changes in the film industry, cinema audiences and wider society.

> In Britain, I'm seen as one of the most commercial directors that Britain has now, when I made *Bhaji on the Beach*, I was kind of an ethnic little something on the side. (Chadha interviewed by *Gay City News*, USA, 2003)

● *Bhaji on the Beach* is a comedy about the problems facing a group of British Asian women living in Birmingham. It shares some of the themes of *Bend It Like Beckham*. The central character is a young woman caught between British and Asian traditions, which are reflected by different generations. A subplot features lesbian characters, a recurring theme also evident in *What's Cooking?*; *Bhaji on the Beach* is stylistically more experimental than Chadha's other films with dream sequences and the influence of 'Bollywood' cinema evident.

● *What's Cooking?* is an American independent film set during the Thanksgiving holiday, following the experiences of families from several different ethnic backgrounds (Jewish, Italian-American, Korean, African-American, Hispanic/Latino). Conflicts in the family groups are generational, cultural and sexual. Stylistically, the film uses a multinarrative form (similar to that in *Love, Actually*) to link and contrast the different families. *What's Cooking?* would make a useful comparative text to examine how ideas about national identity are explored in an American context.

● *Bride and Prejudice* is a Bollywood adaptation of *Pride and Prejudice*. This mixing of the very English world of Jane Austen with Indian culture fits the themes of Chadha's earlier work, analysing the way different cultures are linked while also dramatising the differences. The highly structured society of Austen's characters, the importance of convention, tradition and propriety, also seem similar to the world of the parents in *Bend It Like Beckham*, and there are parallels between Jesminder in that film and Elizabeth Bennett; both are clever and determined, with a spirit of rebellion. *The Sunday Telegraph Magazine* in December 2003 featured *Bride and Prejudice* as its cover story, another example of the mainstream context in which Chadha's films are now read. The critical and commercial reception of the film has been mixed; for an Indian perspective, see http://timesofindia.indiatimes.com, which contains reviews and interviews.

● *I Dream of Jeannie* (USA, 2005), in production at the time of writing, is a big-budget ($10m for special effects alone) remake of the 1960s US TV sitcom. In discussing the character of Jeannie, Chadha suggests the way even this project develops themes relevant to her work; 'She's a Muslim girl, and the story is about Muslims …. The notion of women in burkas on a big Hollywood screen is pretty radical.' (*The Daily Telegraph*, 20 September 2004).

The move to mainstream Hollywood filmmaking raises questions about the options open to British filmmakers: whether to continue making British films with all the attendant problems of finance and distribution or to work for the Hollywood studios. Directors who have made this transition include Alfred Hitchcock, Alan Parker, Ridley Scott, Tony Scott, Danny Boyle, Paul W S Anderson.

● *Bend It Like Beckham*

> I try to provide films that are entertaining and at the same time moving. But with Bend It Like Beckham the inspiration was drawn from wanting to make a wide appealing, commercial British movie, focusing on the themes that I enjoy talking about. I wanted to make a film for the multiplexes of Britain. (Gurinder Chadha)

As this indicates, *Bend It Like Beckham* became a mainstream film triumph, breaking out of the British Asian film category. One way to approach the film is to analyse the reasons for this commercial success.

Discussion points

Students could consider:

● *Bend It Like Beckham* as a mainstream film:
  – It is a coming-of-age drama. Films belonging to this category usually focus on young men; that the central character here is female indicates the kind of gender representation in the film.
  – The film belongs to the genre of comedy drama. The comedy is often found in the unexpectedness of characters' behaviour and situations while the drama comes from conflict.
  – Conflicts in the film are culturally specific but also universal: mothers and daughters, sisters, best friends, romantic relationships.
  – The film seems to be aimed at a youth audience (central character, subject matter, soundtrack), the most frequent filmgoers, but it also has appeal for older generations.
  – The title of the film provided an excellent marketing opportunity and ensured the film immediate recognition among the public.

● Themes of representation, national and cultural identity:
  – Representation of gender: The representation of women is interesting in all Chadha's films. Here gender expectations are subverted through the central theme of sport, and also through the representation of age. Particular emphasis is put on the value of female friendship and achievement.

- Representation of sexuality: Gay themes are explored in the film through two story lines. *Bend It Like Beckham* has been read as a queer film by lesbian audiences due to the subversion of female gender stereotypes.
- Representation of national and cultural identity: Britain is represented as a harmonious multicultural society. The cultural and racial backgrounds of the characters are represented in an unproblematic way; Jesminder's and Jules' arguments with their mothers are the same. Hounslow, the specific multicultural setting, is symbolic of the rest of the country.

● **Worksheet 24: Representation in *Bend It Like Beckham***

Film extracts: 00.7.38–00.11.20 and 00.23–00.26m

Textual analysis is used to discuss the representation of gender, race and culture.

To access worksheets and other online materials go to **www.bfi.org.uk/tfms** and enter User name: **britcin** and Password: **te1511bc**.

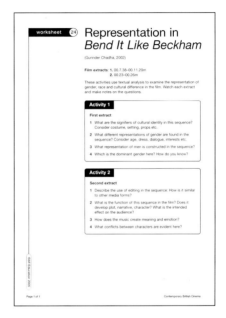

Discussion points

Students could consider:
- The different conflicts between parents and children; Jesminder and her cousins; and Jesminder, Jules and the male football players;
- Representations of Hounslow and British Asian culture;
- How the skill of the female football players is used to construct a positive representation of young women;
- The use of film language; the montage sequence with music soundtrack (Curtis Mayfield 'Move on up'), emphasises the humorous, optimistic and aspirational message;
- Is *Bend It Like Beckham* closest in style and content to the social realist tradition of British cinema?

Case study 3: British cinema and institutions

● Production and distribution in the British film industry

With the injection of UK National Lottery money in the 1990s, things looked bright for the British film industry as film production increased. However, many of the films funded did not get distribution, and therefore exhibition. It became apparent that Britain's lack of a distribution network, controlled by British film companies, has been a major obstacle to a flourishing industry. Criticism of Lottery-funded films focused on the lack of time spent in development: ideas were rushed through, without sufficient attention to the quality of the script.

To explore these issues, this section provides a case study of two institutions which deal with different parts of the production process: FilmFour (producer, distributor) and Working Title (producer). The case study considers:

● The problems of distributing and exhibiting British films;
● Competition with Hollywood;
● The kinds of films that appeal to British audiences;
● Whether the main aim should be to appeal to the domestic or global audience.

What is film distribution?

● A film distributor is the link between film producers and exhibitors (the cinema chains); their aim is to get as many people as possible to see the film on as many cinema screens as possible.
● The distributor markets the film and develops an appropriate advertising campaign.
● To market successfully, the distributor has to target the appropriate audience.
● The distributor needs to create interest in a film; this can be easy if there is a clear 'selling point' such as a star, but harder in the case of low-budget, independent films.
● Distributors employ researchers to track the recognition of the film with the target audience during the campaign.
● The UK has 'major' distributors (affiliated to the Hollywood studios) and independent (unaffiliated) distributors who tend to handle films made outside the major studios.
● In Hollywood in the 1930s and 1940s exhibition was the most financially important part of the filmmaking process; now distribution dominates.

More information about the role of distributors and domestic box office statistics can be found at www.launchingfilms.com.

● FilmFour

In July 2002, FilmFour disbanded; film production was once again overseen by Channel 4 and the budget was cut by two-thirds. (The man chiefly responsible for this was Mark Thompson, who later replaced Greg Dyke as the Director General of the BBC in 2004.) Its role as a distributor was ended. The closing of FilmFour as a standalone film operation seemed to confirm the impossibility of Britain achieving a sustainable film industry. The history of FilmFour exemplifies the specific problems facing British producers and distributors.

History

1982: *The launch of Channel 4.* The broadcaster's remit to address audiences not catered for by other channels was evident in the setting up of Channel Four Films, which commissioned low- to medium-budget films from independent producers, primarily for broadcast on the channel, although some received cinema exhibition. In the 1980s, the films helped to give the channel its distinct identity, promoted diversity in film (through on-screen representations and those involved in production) and explored contemporary social and political problems. The channel's output included *The Ploughman's Lunch* (Richard Eyre, 1983), *Letter to Brezhnev*, *My Beautiful Laundrette*, *Rita, Sue and Bob Too*, *The Draughtsman's Contract* (Peter Greenaway, 1982), *Dance with a Stranger* (Mike Newell, 1984), *Mona Lisa* (Neil Jordan, 1986), *Distant Voices, Still Lives*. Channel Four Films also made investments in co-productions, such as *Paris Texas* (Wim Wenders, USA, 1984).

1992–1997: This period marked an increase in the domestic and international success of British films. Success for the British film industry tends to be cyclical. In the early 1980s the British production company Goldcrest attempted to compete with Hollywood by making big-budget films which would succeed in America. For several years, the company achieved financial and critical success with films including *Chariots of Fire* and *Gandhi*, which both won Oscars, *The Killing Fields* (Roland Joffe, 1984) and *Room with a View*. However the big budgets and poor box-office receipts of *Revolution* (Hugh Hudson, UK/USA, 1985) and *Absolute Beginners* (Julien Temple, 1986) led to the closure of Goldcrest in 1986. The fact that two poorly performing films can hasten the end of a company is indicative of the problems faced by small, independent British producers. They do not have the volume of production or distribution to absorb the loss (effectively, the principle of economies of scale).

In contrast, the American production company Warner Brothers was able to survive a disastrous big-budget flop such as *The Postman* (Kevin Costner, USA, 1997): the cost of production alone was $80m (not including marketing) and the US box-office gross was just over $5m. However, profits made from Warner

Brothers' other films, television channels and music and publishing companies cushioned it. Ultimately, *The Postman* broke even through overseas cinema exhibition, video and DVD distribution.

Channel Four Films was a major contributor to the success of British films in America in the 1990s. *The Crying Game* (Neil Jordan, 1992), with a US box office gross of $62m, and *Four Weddings and a Funeral* (see p 35), both achieved great success in America. The evidence that independent British films could compete internationally (*Four Weddings and a Funeral* took $240m worldwide) was one of the founding strategies of FilmFour. This period was also characterised by a new excitement about British film with the domestic audience, again partly led by Channel 4. Films included: *Shallow Grave* (Danny Boyle, 1994), *Secrets and Lies* (Mike Leigh, 1996) and *Trainspotting*. *Trainspotting* in particular symbolised the kind of alternative, youth-orientated filmmaking which FilmFour planned for the domestic market. In 1997 two important forms of public subsidy were introduced:

- Lottery money distributed via the Arts Council (UK Film Council after 2000, see p24);
- Tax relief. Films under a budget of £15m would qualify for 100% tax write-off. (This was known as Section 48 and was suddenly withdrawn in February 2004. For further discussion of the use of subsidies through tax relief, see Macnab, 2004.)

The effect of this was that production rose to a level not seen since the 1970s.

1998–2002:   The success of Channel Four Films, internationally and domestically, led to the creation of an autonomous film production and distribution company: FilmFour, part of the commercial arm of Channel 4, 4Ventures (which consisted of E4, the FilmFour satellite and cable channels, and Channel 4 websites). These platforms could all operate as exhibitors and promoters of the FilmFour product. With a distribution arm as well as a production base, FilmFour was a unique attempt to integrate the different film processes in Britain. This structure and the type of films that were made and distributed led to comparisons with the American company, Miramax.

FilmFour had a production budget of £32m, twice the budget of Channel Four Films. *East Is East* proved an early success (see p63 for budget and box office), but the fact that this was a 'surprise' hit led some critics to wonder if the new FilmFour really had the necessary understanding of what a British audience was looking for. Within the context of a debate about British cinema, it is interesting that FilmFour's most successful film was one rooted firmly within the tradition of social realism. In 2000, FilmFour made a deal with Warner Brothers to deliver seven films over three years, with budgets of £13m and above. Although compared to Hollywood, this is a small budget, the average cost of a British film at the time was £3m and Channel Four Film's greatest successes had come from films costing less than that.

The film most often referred to as responsible for the demise of FilmFour as a production company is *Charlotte Gray* (Gillian Armstrong, UK/Australia/Germany, 2001). *Charlotte Gray* is an interesting example of an attempt to make a British film with appeal for an international, particularly American, market and, in this way, is similar to the films produced by Goldcrest. Critics of this strategy argued that in trying to please both the domestic and international market, FilmFour ended up doing neither. Many of the films released in 2000 and 2001 achieved neither box-office success nor critical acclaim.

A lesser-known contributor to the end of FilmFour was the Hollywood film, *Death to Smoochy* (Danny DeVito, USA/UK/Germany, 2002) starring Robin Williams and Ed Norton. FilmFour contributed $5m to the production costs of $55m; the film grossed $8m in the US and was only released on video and DVD in the UK.

Budget and box office figures for FilmFour

Film	Budget (£m)	Box office (£m)	Comment
Lucky Break (2000)	4.00	1,254,772	
Charlotte Gray (2001)	14.00	1,567,185	
The Navigators (Ken Loach, 2000)	1.70	900	A drama documentary about the privatisation of the railways, shown on Channel 4 and only had a very limited cinema release.
The Filth and the Fury (Julien Temple, 2000)	0.60	117	A documentary on the Sex Pistols
Once Upon a Time in the Midlands	3.00	494,281	Nottingham set comedy/Western

FilmFour did not just attempt to produce crowd-pleasing genre films, they also invested in films which could be defined as 'typically British' and continued their trademark interest in alternative, or art cinema. The above figures illustrate the competing pressures on national cinema to provide culturally specific films and survive financially; even *Once Upon a Time in the Midlands* which starred well-known actors (Ricky Tomlinson, Rhys Ifans, Robert Carlyle) in an accessible genre made a loss at the box office.

In addition to production, FilmFour also distributed more than 60 films (many of which also had FilmFour investment) including: *Ghost Dog: Way of the Samurai* (Jim Jarmusch, USA, 1999), *Bully* (Larry Clark, USA, 2001), *The Limey* (Steven Soderbergh, USA, 1999) and *Monsoon Wedding* (Mira Nair, India/USA, 2001).

FilmFour played an important role in the distribution of films which British audiences were unlikely to have access to otherwise, to cinemas and on video and DVD. FilmFour also funded FilmFour Lab, whose aim was to develop 'singular' voices through short films and low-budget feature films.

Why did FilmFour fail?

The reasons for the closure of FilmFour as a production company go beyond the box-office failures of *Charlotte Gray* and *Lucky Break*. The parent company 4Ventures had an operating loss of £65m in 2001, of which £5.4m was attributable to FilmFour. As indicated, FilmFour produced and distributed a variety of creative and interesting low- to medium-budget films, few of which were box-office hits, so the few big failures were devastating. At the time of closure, films on the production slate included: *The Lovely Bones*, to be directed by Lynne Ramsay, *Under the Skin* (Jonathan Glazer who also made *Sexy Beast*), *Bright Young Things* (Stephen Fry, 2003) and *Touching the Void* (Kevin MacDonald, 2003). *Touching the Void*, subsequently turned out to be one of the most successful films FilmFour produced, receiving several awards including the Alexander Korda Award (BAFTA) for Best British Film and Best Film at the Evening Standard Awards.

Jeffries (2002) argues that the failure of FilmFour is indicative of the wider failure of British film culture: British audiences love American films. With the ending of FilmFour as an autonomous company, film production returned to Channel 4, with a much reduced budget. Some critics hope that this will mean a return to the individual, experimental filmmaking of the 1980s and 1990s, without pandering to a mass international audience.

Another factor in the end of FilmFour is the increasing globalisation of the market which has meant greater competition from Hollywood:

> In the UK there is no commercially successful model for a stand alone independent film company. (Rob Woodward, Head of 4Venture, quoted in Andrew Pulver, 'End of an Era', The Guardian, 12 July 2002).

● Working Title: 'Independent and British'?

Working Title is currently the most successful British film production company. Set up in 1984, its longevity alone sets it apart. A study of Working Title suggests one strategy for success for the British film industry: making films with American stars to appeal to an international market. But this approach has provoked criticism about the 'mid-Atlantic' nature of the films. Working Title exemplifies the ongoing debate in the British film industry: whether to make culturally specific films which appeal to a limited audience, or broader, generic films with a wider appeal.

History

- 1984: Working Title founded by Tim Bevan and Sarah Radclyffe;
- First investment: £500,000 in *My Beautiful Laundrette*, the first of a series of collaborations with Channel Four Films;
- 15 films produced in the 1980s;
- 1988: Production deal with PolyGram Filmed Entertainment;
- 1991: Working Title sets up a Hollywood office, developing production deals with Tim Robbins (*Bob Roberts*, UK/USA, 1992 and *Dead Man Walking*, UK/USA, 1995) and the Coen brothers (*Fargo*, UK/USA, 1996, *The Big Lebowski*, UK/USA 1998);
- 1992: PolyGram (a European music and media company) buys Working Title. Sarah Radclyffe leaves to set up her own production company and is replaced by the American producer, Eric Fellner;
- 1998: PolyGram is bought by Universal, a Seagram company;
- 2000: Seagram is bought by Vivendi, the French multimedia conglomerate.
- Working Title is now owned by Universal, which is in turn owned by Vivendi.
  - The deal with Universal allows Working Title to greenlight films up to a budget of $35m;
  - WT2, a low-budget, filmmaking arm was set up to encourage new British filmmakers. One of the first films produced was *Billy Elliot* (Stephen Daldry, 1999).

There is no other British film company like Working Title, which retains autonomy in creative decisions but is owned by a conglomerate. The protection of Universal means that Working Title survived the disappointing performance of *Captain Corelli's Mandolin* (John Madden, UK/France/USA, 2000) (budget: £13m, UK box office: £9.8m) in a way that FilmFour was unable to with *Charlotte Gray*.

Some key Working Title films

Film	Budget (£m)	Box office UK(£m)
Bean (1996)	16.2	17,972,562
Elizabeth (1997)	13	5,536,790
Notting Hill (1998)	15	31,006,109
Bridget Jones's Diary (2000)	14	42,007,008
About a Boy (2001)	13.5	16,850, 239
Love, Actually (2004)	30	36,238,777
Wimbledon (2004)	20 (est)	6,886,568

The increase in production budgets for *Notting Hill*, *Bridget Jones's Diary* and *Love, Actually* was not reflected in box-office takings, meaning reduced profits for Working Title. The sequel to *Bridget Jones's Diary*, *Bridget Jones: The Edge of Reason* (Beeban Kidron, 2004), has an even higher budget of about £40m. *Wimbledon* has been one of Working Title's least successful recent films.

Richard Curtis and Working Title: Representations of Englishness

Richard Curtis is a scriptwriter and director who co-wrote *Blackadder* (BBC), *The Vicar of Dibley* (BBC) and produced Rowan Atkinson's one-man stage plays. The films that he has written (*Four Weddings and a Funeral*, *Notting Hill*, *Bridget Jones's Diary* [co-writer]) and written and directed (*Love, Actually*) are synonymous with the Working Title brand and have also been very influential in creating the Hugh Grant star persona. Their popularity has been countered by a critical response, which accuses the films of creating a fantasy world, which bears little relation to contemporary Britain, and relying on sentimentality and stereotypes. The representation of Englishness in these films might be one of the reasons for their success in America. However, US critics were less enthusiastic about *Love, Actually*.

Characteristics of Richard Curtis/Working Title films:

- **Romantic comedies**: All the films follow the conventions of the romantic comedy genre. The multi-stranded narrative of *Love, Actually* follows rom-com conventions most obviously in the affair between the Prime Minister and the tea girl.

- **Happy endings**: Another rom-com convention, the films all have happy endings, where the central couple is (re)united. However, happiness for one character may mean misery for another (Fiona's unrequited love for Charles in *Four Weddings*, the self-sacrifice of Sarah in *Love, Actually*), hinting at a world which isn't as perfect as it initially seems.

- **Climax**: Happy endings come at the last minute and against all odds. They often involve a climactic dash to catch the object of affection before they leave forever (*Four Weddings*, *Notting Hill*, *Bridget Jones*), taken to the extreme in *Love, Actually* with the chase through Heathrow Airport.

- **Belief in true love**: Charles and Carrie (*Four Weddings and a Funeral*), William and Anna *(Notting Hill)* and the Prime Minister and Natalie (*Love, Actually*) are struck by love at first sight.

- **Sentimentality**: The films are often sentimental because of the emphasis on love conquering all, including divisions of class (two stories in *Love, Actually*) and celebrity (*Notting Hill*).

- **Plot twists**: The plots rely on coincidences and unexpected meetings.

- **Humour**: Richard Curtis is associated with witty dialogue, but slapstick and farce also feature, with the comic sidekick/flatmate (*Four Weddings*, *Notting Hill*) fulfilling the role of clown. Swearing is also used for comic effect through its incongruity due to either class (the opening of *Four Weddings*) or age (the child in *Love, Actually*). The self-deprecating style of humour associated with the Hugh Grant persona is also evident in other characters. For example, Paul Bettany's performance in *Wimbledon* draws on Grant's style of delivery.

- **Stars**: Hugh Grant emerged as a star in *Four Weddings* and his star persona has (largely) remained that of the floppy-haired, bumbling Englishman. The choice of co-star in *Four Weddings*, Andie MacDowell, shows how American stars are used to attract American distribution and audiences. This is also evident in the casting of Kirsten Dunst in *Wimbledon*. *Love, Actually* featured an ensemble cast of British and American actors with Hugh Grant as the only 'Hollywood' star.

- **Settings**: The city. Mostly set in London, the city is represented in a highly selective manner. London is shown as a collection of 'villages' (Southwark's Borough in *Bridget Jones's Diary*, Notting Hill in *Notting Hill*,) with the bustle of markets, local restaurants, little traffic and safe streets. Characters tend to live in houses and flats that they could not afford on their earnings (Bridget Jones, Will in *Notting Hill*, Sarah in *Love, Actually*). These aspects add to the fantasy and escapism. Or, is this a realistic representation of what London is like if you are upper middle class?

- **The weather**: Closely linked to setting, the weather is important for creating atmosphere. It often draws on clichés such as the snow falling at Christmas in *Bridget Jones's Diary* or the rain signifying passion at the end of *Four Weddings*. Otherwise, it tends to be beautifully sunny.

- **Representation of race**: The main and supporting characters in these films are white. This has caused some controversy, particularly in the case of *Notting Hill*, which is set in what is actually a multi-ethnic area of West London.

- **Representation of people with disabilities**: Richard Curtis films are some of the very few examples of mainstream cinema which include characters with disabilities who are not defined by them. (David in *Four Weddings*, Bella in *Notting Hill*).

Case studies

● **Worksheet 25: Defining characteristics of Working Title films**

Based on students' knowledge and research into Working Title films, this worksheet asks them to analyse the characteristics of Working Title films and produce a synopsis for their own film.

To access worksheets and other online materials go to **www.bfi.org.uk/tfms** and enter User name: **britcin** and Password: **te1511bc**.

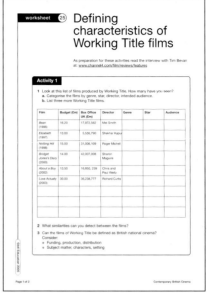

1 of 2 pages

Notting Hill *and* Bridget Jones's Diary

Both these films can be studied in the context of:

● Working Title's style of filmmaking;
● A discussion of definitions of national cinema.

● **Worksheet 26: *Bridget Jones's Diary* and the conventions of Working Title films**
Film extract: 1.20.43m – end of the film (12mins)

Discussion points

Using the factors outlined as a starting point, discuss:

● The use of setting for character and atmosphere: Bridget's flat, the Borough street and the weather;
● Characteristics of Bridget's friends;
● The narrative conventions of the romantic comedy, the climax of the film;

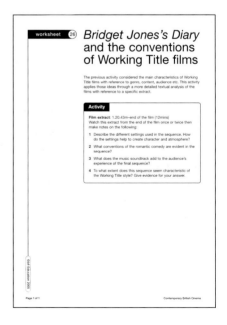

82

- The use of British and American stars;
- Soundtrack; also important as a marketing device;
- The representation of London: the snow, nearly empty streets etc.

- **Worksheet 27: *Notting Hill*
  and issues of representation**
Film extracts: 33.33–39.08m and
00.2.43–04.14m

Notting Hill epitomises the Working
Title signature style through the use of
genre, stars and character. These
sequences illustrate the representation
of London and class found in many of
the films. The first sequence is from
the beginning and the second is a
dinner party to celebrate Honey's
(Will's sister) birthday.

To access worksheets and other online
materials go to **www.bfi.org.uk/tfms**
and enter User name: **britcin**
and Password: **te1511bc**.

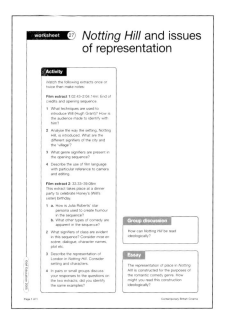

Discussion points

Students could consider:

- The representation of Notting Hill: the way in which signifiers of a 'village' and the city are combined. Does this have an ideological function?
- Use of *mise en scène*: the market, shops, Will's home, dinner party, costume;
- The introduction of the main character: the Hugh Grant star persona;
- Characteristics of Will's friends; appearances, jobs, personalities, signifiers of class, the references to 'lifestyles';
- Whether the film suggests certain values are normal and natural;
- How the film uses the conventions of the romantic comedy;
- Film language, soundtrack;
- Types of humour.

Glossary

Asylum seeker
A person claiming refugee status due to fear of persecution in their own country. The term is increasingly used incorrectly as a synonym for immigrant and pejoratively by sections of the press and political parties.

Auteur/author
A film director with consistent themes and a style which is identifiable across a body of work.

Bollywood
Popular term for the Indian film industry, increasingly problematic and offensive to some filmmakers and audiences.

British Asian
British citizens of South Asian (India, Pakistan, Bangladesh) origin or descent.

British New Wave
Influential period of filmmaking (approximately 1959–63) with a commitment to represent working-class life.

Capitalist ideology
The ideas promoted by the ruling class that present capitalism (the private ownership of capital and means of production for profit, as opposed to state ownership and collective benefit) as the best possible political and economic system. (See Frankfurt School.)

Counter-cinema
Originally associated with European art cinema and feminist filmmaking of the 1960s and 1970s. Characterised by its opposition to the classic narrative and invisible film language conventions of mainstream cinema.

Diaspora/diasporic
Forced dispersal or migration of a particular group from a nation or area to another country, resulting in a diasporic nation, eg Eastern European Jews in the 19th century.

Film collective
A politically motivated group founded on the ideals of equality rather than the hierarchical roles of producer, director etc, which

operates outside the mainstream film industry producing experimental cinema. Originally associated with left-wing political movements of the 1960s and 1970s.

Film noir

Linked to the crime and gangster genres, *film noir* refers to a period of Hollywood filmmaking characterised by a distinctive visual style, created through extreme contrasts of light and dark (low-key lighting) and consistent narrative and character tropes, eg *Double Indemnity* (Billy Wilder, USA, 1944), *Out of the Past* (Jacques Tourneur, USA, 1947).

Frankfurt School

A leftwing academic tradition originating in Germany in the 1920s, which developed an influential critique of capitalism that focused on industries of popular culture as part of the capitalist system. Argued that inequalities survived largely because popular culture encourage passivity.

Immigration

Government policy of allowing entry to and residency in the UK, usually for work (often to fill gaps in the labour market), study or family reasons. Sometimes referred to as economic migration.

Invisible film language/style

A style of mainstream filmmaking which hides, rather than draws attention to, the use of film language/style in order to aid the suspension of disbelief.

Mise en scène

The visual elements of a film, assumed to be under the control of the director, which create meaning for the audience.

Montage

A sequence of brief shots, sometimes linked by fades and dissolves, which compresses time and/or space.

Narrative resolution

The way in which mainstream films resolve the questions raised at the beginning of the narrative.

Realism (social realism)

A film aesthetic which aims to show the world as it is, with the emphasis often on socially marginalised groups.

Refugee

Anyone with a well-founded fear of being persecuted for reasons of race, religion, nationality, membership of a particular social group, or political opinion. A person with refugee status cannot return to their own country.

Representation

The way in which particular groups etc are re-presented in media texts, which can be analysed to asses its social effects.

Tax break

(Legal) tax loophole which means that individuals do not pay tax on money invested in films. It can be used to encourage investment in domestic film, decreasing the need for public funding.

Filmography

A selected list of British films mentioned in this guide. A fuller list of British films can be found at www.bfi.org.uk/tfms.

About a Boy (Chris and Paul Weitz, UK/USA, 2002)
Alfie (Charles Shyer, UK/USA, 2003)
Anita and Me (Metin Huseyin, 2003)
Bandit Queen (Shekhar Kapur, India/UK, 1994)
Bean (Mel Smith, 1996)
Beautiful Thing (Hettie MacDonald, 1996)
Bend It Like Beckham (Gurinder Chadha, 2002)
Bhaji on the Beach (Gurinder Chadha, 1995)
Billy Elliot (Stephen Daldry, 1999)
Bloody Sunday (Paul Greengrass, UK/Ireland, 2002)
Bollywood Queen (Jeremy Wooding, 2002)
Brassed Off (Mark Herman, 1996)
Bride and Prejudice (Gurinder Chadha, 2004)
Bridget Jones's Diary (Sharon Maguire, 2000)
Brothers in Trouble (Udayan Prasad, 1995)
Butterfly Kiss (Michael Winterbottom, 1994).
Calendar Girls (Nigel Cole, 2003)
Chariots of Fire (Hugh Hudson, 1981)
Charlotte Gray (Gillian Armstrong, UK/Australia/Germany, 2001)
Cold Mountain (Anthony Minghella, 2003)
Croupier (Mike Hodges, UK/France, 1998)
Crying Game, The (Neil Jordan, 1992)
Dance with a Stranger (Mike Newell, 1984)
Dirty Pretty Things (Stephen Frears, 2002)
Draughtsman's Contract, The (Peter Greenaway, 1982)
East Is East (Damien O'Donnell, 1998)
Elizabeth (Shekar Kapur, 1997)
Filth and the Fury, The (Julien Temple, 2000)

Four Weddings and a Funeral (Mike Newell, 1994)
Full Monty, The (Peter Cattaneo, 1997)
Gandhi (Richard Attenborough, 1982)
Girl with a Pearl Earring (Peter Webster, 2003)
Gosford Park (Robert Altman, UK/US, 2001)
Handsworth Songs (John Akomfrah, 1986)
House of America (Marc Evans, 1997)
In This World (Michael Winterbottom, 2003)
In Which We Serve (David Lean, 1942)
Iris (Richard Eyre, 2002)
Kevin and Perry Go Large (Ed Bye, 1999)
Ladybird, Ladybird (Ken Loach, 1993)
Last Orders (Fred Schepisi, 2001)
Last Resort (Paul Pawlikowski, 2000)
Lock, Stock and Two Smoking Barrels (Guy Ritchie, 1998)
Loneliness of the Long Distance Runner, The (Tony Richardson, 1962)
Love, Actually (Richard Curtis, 2003)
Magdalene Sisters, The (Peter Mullan, 2002)
Mona Lisa (Neil Jordan, 1986)
Morvern Callar (Lynne Ramsay, 2001)
Mrs Brown (John Madden, 1997)
My Beautiful Laundrette (Stephen Frears, 1985)
My Son the Fanatic (Udayan Prasad, 1997)
Navigators, The (Ken Loach, 2000)
Nil by Mouth (Gary Oldman, 1995)
Notting Hill (Roger Michell, 1998)
Once Upon a Time in the Midlands (Shane Meadows, 2001)
Playing Away (Horace Ove, 1986)
Pressure (Horace Ove, 1975)
Ratcatcher (Lynne Ramsay, 1998)
Saturday Night and Sunday Morning (Karel Reisz, 1960)
Saving Grace (Nigel Cole, 2000)
Secrets and Lies (Mike Leigh, 1996)
Sex Lives of the Potato Men (Andy Humphries, 2004)
Sexy Beast (Jonathan Grazer, 2000)
Shallow Grave (Danny Boyle, 1994)
Shaun of the Dead (Edgar Wright, 2004)
Shopping (Paul Anderson, 1994)
Sliding Doors (Peter Howitt, UK/USA, 1998)
Solomon and Gaenor (Paul Morrison, 2000)
Speak Like a Child (John Akomfrah, 1998)
Sweet 16 (Ken Loach, 2002)
Sylvia (Christine Jeffs, 2003)

24:7 (Shane Meadows, 1997)

24 Hour Party People (Michael Winterbottom, 2001)

28 Days Later (Danny Boyle, UK/US, 2004)

Taste of Honey, A (Tony Richardson, 1961)

Touching the Void (Kevin MacDonald, 2003)

Trainspotting (Danny Boyle, 1996)

Twin Town (Kevin Allen, 1997)

Typically British (Stephen Frears, 1995)

Warrior, The (Asif Kapadia, UK/France, 2001)

Wimbledon (Richard Loncraine, 2004)

Wondrous Oblivion (Paul Morrison, UK/Germany, 2003)

Yma/Nawr [*Still: Here/Now*] (Marc Evans, 2003)

Young Adam (David Mackenzie, UK/France, 2003)

Young Soul Rebels (Isaac Julien, 1991)

Bibliography

K Alexander, 2000, 'Black British Cinema in the 1990s: Going Going Gone' in R Murphy (ed), *British Cinema of the 90s*, Routledge

B Anderson, 1983, *Imagined Communities*, Verso

A Barker, 2001, *Bollywood*, Pocket Essentials

S Bourne, 1998, *Black in the British Frame: Black People in British Film and TV (1896–1996)*, Cassell

G Branston and R Stafford (eds), 1997, *The Media Student's Book*, Routledge

X Brooks, 2000, *Choose Life: Ewan McGregor and the British Film Revival*, Deutsch

G Brown, 1997, 'Paradise Found and Lost: The Course of British Realism' in R Murphy (ed), *The British Cinema Book*, bfi

G Chadha, 2003, 'Call That a Melting Pot?' 11 April, *The Guardian*

A Chrisafis, 2002, 'British Actors Say Outlook Is Bleak In "Institutionally Racist" Film Sector', 26 March, *The Guardian*

R Dyer, 1993, *The Matter of Images*, Routledge

R Dyer, 1999, Stars, *bfi*

P Gilroy, 1987, *There Ain't No Black in the Union Jack: The Cultural Politics of Race and Nation*, Hutchinson

S Hall, 1997, *Representation: Cultural Representation and Signifying Practices*, Open University

J Hallam, 2000, 'Film, Class and National Identity: Re-imagining Communities in the Age of Devolution', in J Ashby and A Higson (eds), *British Cinema, Past and Present*, Routledge

S Hayward (2000), *Cinema Studies: The Key Concepts*, Routledge

W Hewing, 2003, *British Cinema in the 1960s*, bfi

A Higson, 2000, 'The Instability of the National' in J Ashby and A Higson (eds), *British Cinema, Past and Present*, Routledge

A Higson, 1989, 'The Concept of National Cinema' in Screen, Vol 30, no4

J Hill, 2000, 'From the New Wave to 'Brit-grit': Continuity and Difference in Working-class Realism' in J Ashby and A Higson (eds), *British Cinema, Past and Present*, Routledge

J Hill, 1999, *British Cinema in the 1980s*, Clarendon

J Hill, 1997, 'Finding a Form: Politics and Aesthetics in Fatherland, Hidden Agenda and Riff-Raff' in G McKnight (ed), *Agent of Challenge and Defiance: The Films of Ken Loach*, Flicks Books

J Hill, 1997, 'British Cinema as National Cinema' in R Murphy (ed) *The British Cinema Book*, bfi

J Hill, 1986, *Sex Class and Realism, bfi*

S Jeffries, 2002, 'FilmFour's Blurred Vision' 10 July, *The Guardian*

L Johnson (ed), 1997, *Talking Pictures, Interviews with Contemporary British Filmmakers, bfi*

S Johnston, 1985, 'Charioteers and Ploughmen' in N Roddick and M Auty (eds), *British Cinema Now, bfi*

H Kolawole, 2003, 'Screen Test', 18 August, *The Guardian*

M Kuhn, 2002, *One Hundred Films and a Funeral*, Thorogood

M Landy, 2000, 'The Other Side of Paradise: British Cinema from an American Perspective' in J Ashby and A Higson, (eds), *British Cinema: Past and Present*, Routledge

M Lawson, 2003, 'It's Magic', 13 November, *The Guardian*

S Lay, 2003, *British Social Realism: From Documentary to Brit Grit,* Wallflower Press

J Leigh, 2003, *The Cinema of Ken Loach: Art in the Service of the People*, Wallflower Press

M Luckett, 2000, 'Image and Nation in 1990s British Cinema' in R Murphy (ed), *British Cinema of the 90s*, Routledge

G Macnab, 2004, ' Break Dancing' in *Sight and Sound*, May, vol 14, issue 5.

G Macnab, 2002, 'Five Years of Flack' 25 October, *The Guardian*

C Monk, 2000, 'Underbelly UK: The 1990s Underclass Film, Masculinity and the Ideologies of "New" Britain' in J Ashby and A Higson (eds), *British Cinema: Past and Present*, Routledge

R Murphy (ed), 2000, *British Cinema of the 90s,* Routledge

R Murphy (ed), 1997, *The British Cinema Book*, bfi

R Murphy, 1985, 'Three Companies: Boyd's Co, Handmade and Goldcrest' in N Roddick and M Auty (eds), *British Cinema Now*, bfi

J Pines, 1997, 'British Cinema and Black Representation', in R Murphy, (ed) *The British Cinema Book*, bfi

A Pouries, 2000, 'Filmmaking is a Business Like Any Other', 25 August, *The Guardian*

N Roddick, 1985, 'If the United States Spoke Spanish…', in N Roddick and M Auty (eds), *British Cinema Now, bfi*

I Sinclair, 2001, 'Last Resort' in *Sight and Sound*, March

P Sorlin, 2000, 'From *The Third Man* to *Shakespeare in Love*: Fifty Years of British Success on Continental Screens' in J Ashby and A Higson (eds), *British Cinema, Past and Present*, Routledge

R Stafford, 2001, 'Where's the Black in the Union Jack?', in the *British Cinema Reader* at www.itpmag.demon.co.uk

S Street, 2002, *Transatlantic Crossings: British Feature Films in the USA*, Continuum

D Strinati, 1995, *An Introduction to the Theories of Popular Culture*, Routledge

P Wickham, 2003, *Producing the Goods? UK Film Production Since 1991*, bfi

P Willemen, 1989, 'The Third Cinema Question: Notes and Reflections', in J Pines and P Willemen (eds), *Questions of Third Cinema*, bfi

R Williams, 1970, 'Recent English Drama' in B Ford (ed), *The Pelican Guide to English Literature 7: the Modern Age,* Penguin

L Young, 1996, *Fear of the Dark: 'Race', Gender and Sexuality in the Cinema,* Routledge

Further reading

R Armstrong, 2005, *Understanding Realism, bfi*

M Bernink and P Cook (eds), 1999, *The Cinema Book*, bfi

E Dyja (ed), annual, *The BFI Film Handbook*, bfi

D Fleming (ed), 2000, *Formations: A 21st Century Media Studies Textbook*, Manchester University Press

J Hill and P Church Gibson (eds), 1998, *The Oxford Guide to Film Studies*, Oxford University Press

J Nelmes (ed), 1996, *An Introduction to Film Studies*, Routledge

Sight and Sound, film journal, bfi

G Turner, 1988, *Film as Social Practice*, Routledge

Also see the bfi National Library 16+ study guides:

Contemporary British Cinema at http://www.bfi.org.uk/nationallibrary/collections/16+/britishcontemp/index.html

60s British Cinema at http://www.bfi.org.uk/nationallibrary/collections/16+/british60s/

Useful websites

http://www.bbc.co.uk – the BBC website includes sections on film, articles, interviews etc

http://www.bbc.co.uk/asiannetwork – includes discussions of Indian cinema

http://www.bfi.org.uk – the BFI website with links to its library facility and study resources etc, including a section of online reviews and features from their film journal, *Sight and Sound*

http://www.channel4.com – Channel 4's website, which has an extensive
    section on film, with a special emphasis on world cinema
http://englishandmedia.co.uk – the website of the English and Media Centre
    which offers a range of useful resources
http://www.filmunlimited.co.uk – *The Guardian*'s film pages
http://www.imdb.co.uk – Internet Movie Database, extensive reviews, details
    on cast, crew, production etc
http://www.launchingfilms.com – the Film Distributors' Association (FDA)
    website covering distribution of films in Britain, with detailed examples,
    box-office figures etc.
http://www.luxonline.org.uk – history and current practice in independent film
    and video
http://www.screenonline.org.uk – detailed education site on British film and
    television history
http://www.timeout.com/film – *Time Out*'s website, with film reviews and
    features
http://ukfilmcouncil.org.uk – the website of the UK Film Council
www.ukfilmcouncil.org.uk/shorts and www.animateonline.org for more
    information on making short films

Acknowledgements

I would like to thank my editors, Vivienne Clark and Wendy Earle, who were
always available to give expert advice and encouragement; Alex Cox and
Chris Chandler for agreeing to be interviewed and for the time and thought
they put into the process; Doreen Casey and Jerry Slater for their detailed
reading and helpful comments throughout.

Special thanks to Farid for technical (and other) support.